On A Ghostly Winter's Night
By Winter Balefire

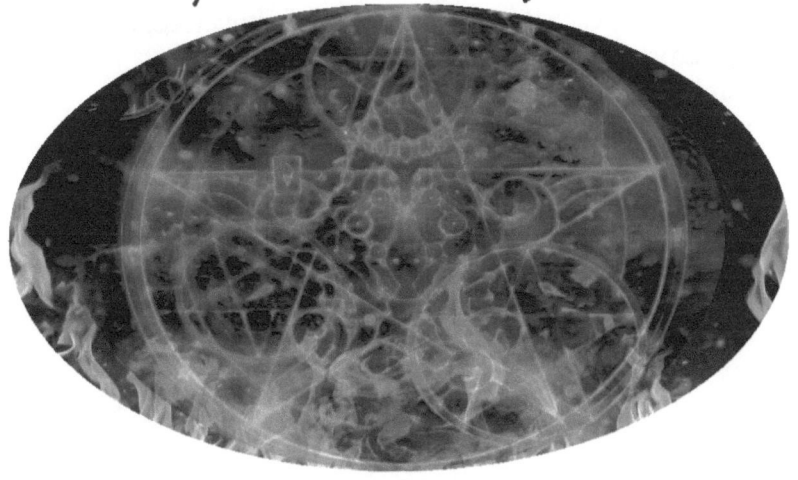

Hauntingly Edited By Cindy Calloway

Table of Contents

Section 3 Urban Legends

Section 4 Paranormal

Foreword

This book is meant for educational and entertainment purposes only. Some rituals and magical workings are described as dangerous and are not meant to be used as a guide, nor to be re-created in any way. There are articles contained in this book which were written several years ago, before some advancements in paranormal research equipment as well as movie adaptations of certain topics existed. Each piece is just a brief description and history, most of these topics could make an entire book by themselves. Some pieces are written from my own personal perspective and experience. Everyone has a right to their beliefs and I in no way wish to make anyone feel their path is wrong. Please keep an open mind and heart. Thank you.

Winter Balefire

Pseudosynth Press Publishing does not and will not claim responsibility for any misdeeds or harm done to anyone living or dead while performing any acts from this book.

Jackie Siefert-Pappas, CEO Pseudosynth Press Publishing

Acknowledgement:

I would like to extend a very special thank you to C.G. Blade and Jackie Siefert-Pappas at Pseudosynth Press for their undying support in bringing my passions to life, as well as Cindy Calloway for her amazing support and editing talent. I'd also like to thank PaganPages.org and Paranormal Underground magazine and radio for allowing me to take my first steps as a Paranormal & Occult researcher.

Dedicated to everyone who has worked tirelessly to teach, explain, and explore all that is unseen.

Section 1

Lore

A Thin Veil

Towards the end of October, it seems that everyone has ghosts on their mind with Halloween just around the corner. Many traditions and superstitions have carried over for many years. Some we have barely modified and some have taken on a life of their own. Most people carry on these old traditions without knowing how or why they came to be. Even for those who do not believe in the paranormal, Halloween turns almost everyone superstitious for one night.

Now vs Then

The holiday we celebrate today is a large blend of different beliefs, religions, and folklore that accumulated over the years. The Celtic belief, over 2,000 years ago, was the night before their new year, November 1st, also known as All Hallows Day, the veil between the living and the dead was very thin. On October 31st, they celebrated Samhain. The Celts believed that on this night the dead would return to Earth and potentially damage their crops. They also believed that druids would return and share knowledge about the future. To celebrate, the Celts would build huge bonfires and dress up in animal skins.

Later, around 43 A.D., the Romans combined their festivals with the Celtic celebrations. One Roman festival honored the Roman Goddess of fruit and trees, Pomona, whose symbol was the apple. This is one explanation for the tradition of bobbing for apples occurring at many Halloween parties today.

Depending on the culture and traditions, this Holiday has always been about either communicating with or warding off spirits. The belief that this is the best time for spirit interaction has been consistent for thousands of years.

During the second half of the nineteenth century, immigrants came over to America and helped to popularize what we now call Halloween, mixing many Irish and English traditions.

Stingy Jack

The tradition of the Jack-o'-lantern came to us from Ireland. Originally, using turnips since pumpkins did not exist in Ireland, faces were carved into the turnip, and a lighted ember was placed inside to ward off spirits. The name Jack-o'-lantern comes from an old Irish tale of a man named Stingy Jack. This man was despised for being a liar and a cheat. He was so skilled at trickery one day he managed to trick the Devil into climbing a tree. Once the Devil was up the tree, Jack placed crosses at the bottom, knowing the Devil could not go near the crosses. He was stuck and Jack made him promise that he would not take his soul when he died. When finally promised, Jack removed the crosses. When Jack's time finally came, he was denied entrance into heaven due to his trickery and thievery so Jack was sent to Hell. The Devil kept his promise and denied Jack entrance as well. With nowhere to go, Jack was given an ember from the fires of Hell to light his way through the darkness of the in between. He had a turnip with him, so he carved out the center and placed the ember inside. Once brought to America, pumpkins were used instead of turnips.

Trick or Treat

Since many believed ghosts walked among us on this night, they would go out disguised as spirits to blend in with the ghosts. The tradition of trick or treating is also an import from Europe, during the All Souls Day celebration in England, poor citizens would beg for food and money. Families would give them pastries called "Soul Cakes" in exchange for a promise they would pray for their dead relatives. The Church welcomed this practice and quickly replaced the older tradition of leaving wine and food out for roaming spirits with the newer tradition.

Return and Tell the Future

The belief of the dead returning was so strong it wasn't uncommon for people to set the dinner table in hopes of welcoming back a deceased family member. Food and candles were left on doorsteps and along the roads for the spirit to find its way. Many forms of divination were performed on this night as well, since the veil was so thin some hoped for a glimpse of their future.

There was a belief many years ago that a young woman should name a hazelnut for each of her suitors, and then toss them one by one into the fire. The nut that completely burned to ashes, without popping or exploding, was the one named for her future husband. Young women would also peel apples and toss the peel over their shoulder to reveal the initials of their true love. Scrying was also popular on Halloween night. Participants would drop egg yolks into a bowl of water and peer into it, or stand in front of a mirror in a dark room holding a candle. Staring long enough into the mirror would bring the vision of a face over your shoulder.

Keeping the Traditions

Many Pagans still celebrate Samhain and honor the old ways, keeping it alive. The Witches' New Year will soon be upon us and for one night, many people of many different backgrounds will celebrate. Though spirits and superstitions are the center, it is also a symbol that wherever there is death there is always new life. The circle will always continue.

Japanese Ghost Lore

Japanese culture is rich in tradition and lore. Many known ghost stories are passed down from generation to generation. Some of these stories may have been created to ensure proper curfew or to teach respect but there is always the question; how many of these tales are rooted in truth?

After Death?

The Japanese Shinto believe that after death a human becomes a spirit with two sides, one good and one evil. These spirits are believed to be everywhere, in water, trees, mountains, and wind. Buddhists believe the way a person behaves while living would determine how they will spend the afterlife. They would go either to the "pure land" or the "Land of the Dead", like Hell. There are also certain prayers and rituals to ensure proper passing of a spirit due to the belief that a spirit starts out angry and confused.

Yurei

A Yurei, or ghost, is believed to haunt the place it once lived and torment the people responsible for any ill feelings it carried during its human life, such as jealousy or envy. These Yurei are often wearing what they were buried in, and any wounds that may have caused their death will be just as visible. A person must pray that the soul of the dead can ascend and be released from its suffering. Without proper funeral rights, they cannot pass on.

Weeping Rocks

Recurring themes in these legends are angry and vengeful ghosts of women who experienced cruelty while they were alive. There is a road between Tokyo and Kyoto known as the "Rocks that Weep". It is said that a woman traveled down that road to meet her husband late one night. The legend says she was attacked by thieves and murdered. Her blood spilled onto the rocks and now these rocks are believed to contain her spirit.

Buruburu

The Buruburu is a ghost believed to inhabit graveyards, forests or any dark quiet location. The name translates to "the sound of shivering" and it will appear to you as a harmless elderly person. The spirit then attaches itself to you; therefore, you'll feel shivers down your spine, and it'll fill you with intense fear, sometimes resulting in heart failure.

Ikiryo

The Ikiryo is a type of spirit that comes from a living person. When someone feels intense emotions like hatred or love, their spirit is believed to leave their body and travel on its own. They will either attempt to attach to the person they love or curse the one they hate.

Tanuki & Kitsune

Humans are not the only ones mentioned. Fox and raccoon are often seen as exhibiting magical abilities. They can be many things; tricksters, frighteners, misleaders and they can even be positive omens at times. The Tanuki is a small furry creature believed to be able to transform into something much more frightening. It is said to become something described as a one-eyed demon who uses nature (earthquakes, lightening) to claim victims. Another popular creature is the Kitsune, a fox with shape shifting abilities. Usually these creatures shift into beautiful women who seduce and even possess men and lead them to their demise.

Bakechochin

There are even stories of inanimate objects containing ghosts. The Bakechochin is a lantern thought to contain the spirits of those who died with hatred and malice in their hearts. The lantern has some human qualities with its long tongue and wild piercing eyes. The spirits living inside will immediately attack anyone who dares to light the lantern.

Many of these stories, in their own bizarre way, promote peaceful living. Warning us all to stay away from hate, jealousy, lust, and all the similar things viewed as evil or sinful throughout the world. The personification of emotions is a popular theme and a memorable way to teach lessons. However, many of these entities and their legends are so ancient the origins have become distorted over the centuries. Yet they are powerful enough to persist and continue to invoke fear from the most modern and advanced cultures.

Mirrors; Superstition and Lore

Whether a believer in the paranormal or not, there is one item every single one of us has that's been surrounded with superstition and ghostly stories for centuries. It's in our homes, our cars, and we even carry it with us. The item I am referring to is a mirror.

Mirrors and Mythology

Perhaps this all started in Greek mythology with the story of Narcissus. The story tells of an extremely good-looking man who was the son of Cephissus, a river god, and Leiriope, a nymph. He was admired by all but would always reject any advances. One-day Narcissus saw his own reflection in a pond and fell deeply in love; Ameinias, who was rejected by Narcissus, may have brought this on. Ameinias ordered the Gods to punish him. There are a few variations to this story, one tells of Narcissus drowning while trying to touch the reflection, another that he did not drink due to fear of harming the reflection and simply wasted away. Regardless, he met his demise due to self-obsession and to this day the term Narcissist is used for anyone who shares the trait. How does this involve the paranormal? Well, this story was also used as a warning that seeing your own reflection is like seeing your own soul and gazing too long may bring consequences.

Mirrors and Divination

Reflective surfaces and mirrors have also been used for Scrying, one of the oldest forms of divination. John Dee, an astrologer, occultist, and consultant to Queen Elizabeth I, used a black obsidian mirror for scrying. It is believed that this technique allows you to see visions and answers to questions by gazing upon the surface. There have always been two main theories behind mirrors that seem to be universal; that they reflect the soul and can tell the future.

Superstitions and Urban Legends

Though there are some good superstitions behind mirrors such as if a couple first catches sight of each other in a mirror they will have a happy union, or a young woman can see her true love if she sits in front of a mirror while eating an apple and brushing her hair. There are primarily cautionary tales and bad omens associated with mirrors. We have all heard the warning if you break a mirror you will have seven years bad luck. So, why seven years? The Romans believed that life renewed itself every seven years, they believed if a person were in bad health their image would cause the mirror to break and they would have to live with the curse until the seven-year mark and their life would be renewed. There is also the theory that if a mirror broke and your reflection became distorted, part of your soul would break as well.

One of the most popular and disturbing superstitions involving mirrors is one that is still practiced today and many of us have probably seen it in recent movies or television series. There is a belief that when a person passes away all mirrors in the home should be covered or turned around due to the fear that the soul will become confused and trapped in the mirror. There is a similar warning to cover or reverse mirrors before bed because some believe your soul can wander at night. In 17th century Europe, it was common to wear tiny mirrors to help guard against the Evil Eye. Just as a mirror can reflect and redirect it is also believed to be an easy portal for the spirit world. The popular urban legend of Bloody Mary is probably the most well-known warning behind this theory, a vengeful spirit that can only be summoned while staring into a mirror, the legend states that she will drag whoever has summoned her back into the mirror with her.

A New Mirror Ritual

A new mirror ritual has come to the surface recently called The Dark Reflection Ritual. The concept is to break a mirror with the intent of releasing the energy held within it, if you survive the night, you will have amazing luck. The belief is the older the mirror the higher the energy contained within the glass. The ritual instructs you to begin at sundown but no later than six hours before dawn. Breathe onto the mirror until it fogs to put your energy into the mirror. You are then instructed to light a candle and hold it to the glass until a small section is blackened, then blow out the candle. Next is breaking the mirror and allowing the energy within to be released. Remember, the older the mirror the higher the energy and the greater the risk. Your luck will get increasingly worse as the night progresses. If you survive until dawn, you will have an equal amount of good fortune. This is not something I recommend attempting but you can research the ritual and read the experiences of others.

There are many superstitions, theories and warnings but the reality is we use mirrors every single day and never really stop to think about any of this. These objects that hang in our homes are more than just decorative, they were believed to reflect our souls and our future. Just a little something to think about the next time you catch your reflection, just don't be too narcissistic and all will be well.

Protection Against Witches?

A Witch was possibly one of the most popular scapegoats in history. Any illness, poverty or misfortune was immediately thought to be caused by Witches. Some were certain these powerful beings were out there just waiting to wreak havoc with potions and curses. So naturally, one had to seek out ways in which to protect themselves from such evil.

Witch Bottles

Witch Bottles date back to the late 16th and 17th century in England and America. The idea behind these bottles was to help someone who believed a curse was placed upon them. The victim of the curse would fill a bottle with sharp objects such as bent pins or needles as well as something that signified the victim such as a drop of their blood or fingernails. Next, the bottle is filled with their urine to symbolize the Witch's bladder. Other variations used stones, thread, feathers, seawater and so on. The contents were as personal as the victim needed them to be. Once prepared, the bottle was corked and either placed in a secret spot in the home, burned or buried. There was a belief that if it were tossed in the fire and destroyed, the curse would be lifted. Some felt keeping the contents intact would cause stress and irritation to the Witch and they would be forced to lift the curse to ease their torment.

Hag Stones

In southwest England, hag stones were a popular tool for protection. These were stones that had a natural hole through them. They would be hung in doorways or windows to protect the home and ensure the children would not be taken by Witches. Some would hang them above the bed to prevent a hag from sitting on their chest at night causing "old hag syndrome" or, what we now know as sleep paralysis. These stones would also be tied around the necks of horses to prevent them from being stolen. Another popular theory was that if you looked through the hole in the stone you could see someone for who or what they truly were, see through any glamour spells and even see other inhuman entities that may be roaming. Hag Stones could only be used by the one who found it or if it were given as a gift with love.

Horseshoes

One of the most widely recognized good luck charms is the horseshoe. It was believed that the iron in the shoe could help to repel Witches and demons. According to European folklore, Witches cannot pass over cold iron. The horseshoe must be placed with the pointed ends facing down to repel evil. They were placed in doorways to prevent these entities from entering the home, placed above the bed to prevent nightmares and hung in chimneys to stop Witches from finding their way inside. When a horseshoe was placed with the pointed side up, this was to prevent good luck from spilling out.

Witches' Seats

In the Channel Islands, you may still be able to see small ledges near the chimneys of certain dwellings. Some will tell you the purpose of these ledges was to keep rainwater from damaging the thatched roof. However, others knew these to as Witches' seats. There was a belief that Witches met every Friday night and would have a long flight back across the islands. Of course, these Witches needed a place to rest hence the purpose of the Witch seat. If the seat was not available, the Witch would become angry and possibly invade the home, bringing chaos.

Witch Marks

Apotropaic marks, also known as Witch marks, were popular in medieval homes and churches. These marks were placed near doorways, windows, and chimneys as protection against Witches and demons. Either carved in stone or made by the torching of a candle flame, these marks consisted of pentagrams, compasses, the letters V and M for the Virgin Mary, and overlapping lines and mazes known as demon traps. The belief was that evil entities were drawn to these lines and would remain stuck following the endless pattern.

We have come a long way in how we view modern Witches, though I feel we still have a long way to go.

History of Séances

The word séance is French and literally translates to seat, sitting, or session. When we hear the word séance, we think of people sitting around a table in a dimly lit room, while a spirit medium attempts to contact the deceased. Usually those in mourning seeking closure seek these experiences.

How Did Séances Start?

One of the first widely documented accounts of a séance was in 1848 with Kate and Margaret Fox. These sisters said they were frightened by loud knocking and banging sounds in their New York home. One-day Kate decided to ask the source of these noises to knock in response when she snapped her fingers. This test was successful and the girls formed a system with the spirit that gave them yes or no answers. Soon they convinced others they were communicating with the spirit of a man that had been murdered in their home. The story became widely known and the girls now had an audience. They began to hold popular séances around 1850 and this was believed to be the start of the Spiritualist movement. Later in 1888, Maggie admitted that the knocking sounds had been staged, but many held onto the idea that these séances were legitimate ways to communicate with the dead.

Spirit Cabinets

When this form of spirit communication became popular, spirit mediums began to use "spirit cabinets". Either these were actual pieces of furniture or the medium would sit behind a curtain. Usually the medium was bound to a chair, with items such as musical instruments placed at their feet. During the session, ghostly hands and faces would appear through a hole in the cabinet or through the curtain and the instruments would begin to play. Upon opening the cabinet or pulling the curtain, the audience would see the still bound medium, proving it was actual spirit communication.

Table Tilting & Automatic Writing

Other popular practices during a séance were table tilting and automatic writing. A group of people, usually 4 or 5 did table tilting. Usually there were several sessions before anything would occur. Each person would sit with his or her hands flat on a table. When this practice was successful, the table would vibrate or move and knocking sounds would be heard.

Automatic writing was performed by a medium during a trance or an altered state of consciousness. The medium would write out words or sentences, apparently messages from the spirit. This was allowing the medium to be used as a tool for the spirit to communicate through, a dangerous practice to say the least. The practices of table tilting and automatic writing were believed to be more of an act of the subconscious and a way to tap into the psychic energy of the living.

A Haunting Profit

Unfortunately, with the popularity of séances came many frauds. A dark room and a few simple magic tricks accompanied by wigs and make-up were effective ways to convince an audience and make money. Some mediums would hide wigs and make-up in their seats for a quick change while the participants were waiting with closed eyes. Balloons had faces painted on them to create a floating apparition and objects were tied with fishing line so they would appear to levitate. The spirit cabinet made a wonderful hiding place for any escape artist to make their session seem real. However not all mediums were frauds.

A Magician to Debunk the Magic

Soon scientists, and even some magicians, would come to check the authenticity of the session and ensure there were no illusions planned. These were, in a way, the first paranormal investigators. One of my favorite stories of séance debunking involves Mr. Harry Houdini himself. His training in magic allowed him to expose frauds. He would often attend sessions in disguise with a reporter and a police officer. He wrote about his experiences in his book 'A Magician Among Spirits'. Before Houdini's death, he and his wife Bess agreed that if his spirit would ever return he would utter the words "Rosabelle Believe", this was from a play Bess performed in when the couple first met, and the name was engraved inside of her ring. Houdini passed away on October 31st, 1926. Bess held séances every Halloween for an entire decade but Houdini never appeared. The practice is continued with magicians throughout the world to this day.

The Devil's Hour

A few weeks back I awoke in the middle of the night, not unusual for me but the sight that greeted me was quite unusual. I saw a figure, it seemed to be a woman, but vey gaunt, downright skeletal. She had no eyes, just empty sockets, and what struck me most is she seemed sad, her head slightly down, and I sensed she was mourning. I assumed I was dreaming, I blinked my eyes but she didn't go away. Then I watched her slowly dissipate into nothing. I looked at the clock; it was just after 3 A.M, also known as "Dead Time" or "The Devil's Hour".

What is Dead Time?

Dead time is the time around 3 A.M when it is believed the barrier between our world and the spirit world is broken. There is a theory that entities can easily communicate with us during this time but what makes this time so different from any other time? There are a few theories, depending on whom you ask.

Why the Devil's Hour?

The theory that 3 A.M is the Devil's hour comes from the belief that it is the direct opposite of the time Jesus was crucified, which was thought to be 3 P.M. Some feel that demonic entities and the Devil himself can rise at this hour to torment the living. Just as a demonic entity would flip a crucifix, imagine it like a flipping of the clock.

Is this the Witching Hour?

Answers vary about this topic. The Witching Hour is usually associated with midnight. There were old beliefs that this was when magic was at its most powerful and it could be practiced under the safety of darkness, away from the judgement of skeptics and non-believers. We all remember the old tales that Witches worked with "the devil" so this may be why the Witching Hour and the Devil's Hour have been used interchangeably as the years passed.

What is really going on?

Our bodies go through stages as we prepare to go to sleep. First, our minds relax as we begin to drift off. Then there is a stage in between waking and sleeping, before we reach REM, that we are most likely to be open to communication with spirits. At this stage, we are not processing rational thought, therefore we are not in the mindset to convince ourselves what we are seeing, or hearing isn't real. Another interesting theory is the pineal gland in our brain that helps produce the sleep hormone melatonin is directly connected to our "third eye" chakra. Consequently, what this means is, our inner psychic is ready to receive messages just as our inner skeptic is quieted. These theories all support the belief that spirits really are trying to communicate with us at this hour. For the side of the skeptic, since our body's cycle through the stages of sleep, some may wake up at 3 A.M simply because that's just the sleep stage we are in at that time.

Finally, for those who are going to sleep believing something creepy or paranormal is going to happen, this makes you more prone to witness something creepy or paranormal. Every shadow and noise can mean something if you're looking for it to mean something. However, I prefer to believe that if you wake up in the middle of the night feeling as if someone is staring at you, there very well may be someone doing just that. Sweet dreams.

Victorian Mourning Rituals

The Victorian Era, 1837 – 1901, brought us some of the most interesting rituals when it came to ways to honor the dead and ensuring the proper release of the spirit. Due to tuberculosis, pneumonia, and other infections, death came often. Unfortunately, a high number of children also passed, some before their first birthday.

When Death Occurred

When a death occurred, the mirrors in the home were covered to ensure the spirit of the deceased wasn't trapped or confused upon leaving the body. If a mirror in the home fell and broke, it was considered a sign that another death was about to occur. The clocks were stopped at the exact time of death; it was believed to be bad luck if this ritual was not performed. The body was watched over every waking minute, hence the term "wake". A wake lasted 3 – 4 days and served a couple of purposes; it allowed family appropriate travel time to visit the deceased and it ensured the person was actually dead and not just in a coma. Flowers and candles were used to hide any unpleasant odors since the practice of embalming had not yet caught on. A wreath of laurel tied with black ribbon was hung on the front door to alert passers by a death had occurred.

Post Mortem Photography

Post-mortem photography was also a popular practice. The invention of the daguerreotype made it easier for families to have photographs of loved ones when they could not afford to have a portrait painted. The deceased were often posed to seem more life-like, propped up with their eyes opened. Children were represented as being in a deep sleep holding their favorite toy. Unfortunately, at times, this was the only photograph mothers would have of their children. Later photographs would depict a more honest image of the deceased in their coffin.

Preventing a Haunting

When the body was removed from the home, it was a common practice to carry the body out feet first. This was to ensure the spirit would not look back and beckon a living family member to join them. Family portraits were often turned face down to prevent possession from the deceased.

Those in mourning would wear all black and non-reflective materials. Some women would wear mourning attire for up to two years. The length of mourning often differed depending on if they were mourning a spouse, child, or other family member. Many wore rings and lockets with a piece of hair that belonged to the deceased. The hair was the one part that didn't change with time so it was the perfect way to remember a loved one.

Listen For the Bells

Usually after four days, it was time to bury the body. Grave robbing was common practice, especially by doctors who needed fresh cadavers for dissection classes, so the graves were often bricked over. There was still a huge fear of burying someone alive so many graves were built with a security system. A bell was placed above the grave with a chain extending down into the coffin. If a person was buried alive they could ring the bell and be removed from their grave. Someone was required to stay in the cemetery to listen for the bells and keep an eye open for grave robbers. There were rumors that this is where the terms "graveyard shift", "Saved by the bell", and "dead ringer" originated from but sadly this is not true. These terms all came about for other reasons despite how fitting they seem to be for this era.

Superstitions

Many superstitions came along with this time as well. Many believed it was bad luck to meet a funeral procession head on and it was recommended to turn around. If this was not an option, they must bow their head and hold on to a button until the procession passed. Many today still honor this tradition. Another common belief was never to wear anything new to a funeral, especially shoes. Tracking the dirt from a cemetery was considered bad luck, an invitation of death and inviting the restless spirits into your home.

What Does It Mean to Be a Witch?

In this current day and age, modern advancements seem to be limitless. We are doing great things with art, technology, medicine, and science. Diversity is everywhere and people (for the most part) are willing to learn about different cultures and beliefs, though different from their own. However, tell someone you're a Witch and you may get a reaction as if it were the 1600s all over again.

A View on Witches Past & Present

I do have to admit that Witches are more widely accepted than even a decade ago, yet I still come across a misinformed soul quite often. Old folklore and modern media have given us images of old hags in pointy hats, hovering over cauldrons, flying on a broom and turning people into toads. Many don't even realize a Witch could be their neighbor, a teacher or doctor; ordinary looking people who don't wear pointy hats or bring curses upon those who cross them. Witches became more widely known when the religion of Wicca became popular in modern culture. However, some view the two as different though it is widely debated.

Is a Witch a Wiccan or Vice Versa?

The confusion starts with the definition of the word "Witch" that states it is Old English of Wicca for masculine and Wicce for feminine. These words changed and morphed over time to form the word Witch, mostly associated with female practitioners, though male Witches do exist and some do not like to be called Warlocks. A male Witch is called a Witch. A warlock, to some, is an offensive term because it describes someone who broke the rules of the Craft or an oath of a Coven and is now an outcast. Subsequently, this original definition leads people to think the word Witch and Wicca or interchangeable. The best way I can describe the difference is a Witch practices Witchcraft, a Wiccan is part of the religion of Wicca. So not all Wiccans are Witches and not all Witches are Wiccans. However, some Wiccans also practice Witchcraft and therefore call themselves Witches. I know it can seem confusing. Some argue the intent of a Witch and a Wiccan are different. Wiccans honor the Lord and the Lady (God and Goddess) while not all Witch's include deities in their craft. The ways in which one practices are vast and there really is no defined way to do so, however there are rules that all, whether Witch or Wiccan, understand.

What Are the Rules?

The one rule everyone has heard of is the rule of three. This is a very widely understood rule that whatever you do will return to you with three times the intensity. Some simply call this Karma. Whatever you practice, if you intend harm, harm will come to you. There are some Witches who believe it is within their right to practice curses as a way of helping karma along. I personally do not believe in this but must respect a Witch's choice of practice. We also have a mutual respect for nature. We understand the power in the elements and treat them with great care. Every tree, animal, insect, and body of water matters. Our whole being is connected to nature, we are as one, therefore, respect nature, respect yourself.

So, There Are No Pointy Hats, Cauldrons or Brooms?

During the turn of the century, artists started drawing Witches with pointy hats for children's fairy tales. The hat may have been an adaptation of the fictional wizard hat or as a symbol of a wise person. There is a theory the brim of the hat was added to appear more suitable for women. Witches do use cauldrons because many different plants, oils and herbs are used in the practice, though some just use a saucepan on a stove. Brooms are used as well, many Witches have a particular broom that is used as a symbol of sweeping away negative energy when blessing a new house or workspace, though unfortunately none of them fly.

How Did Witchcraft Get Associated with Devil Worship?

The easiest way to answer this without getting too deep into religion and different belief systems is simply to state it is a misunderstanding. God and the Devil are from Christian belief systems. Witches have a different set of beliefs. There is good and evil, just different manifestations. In addition, the five-pointed star, the pentagram, played a big part as well. One belief is the pentagram points symbolize the four elements earth, air, fire and water. The fifth point symbolizes the Spirit. This symbol has been used in many different cultures for many reasons. The Church of Satan uses the five-pointed star but inverted, again not the only ones to do this, and it is said to represent a goat's head. There are also many horned deities in Pagan religions and practices. Pagan is simply an umbrella term used to cover beliefs that are not of the main religious sects. So unfortunately, some people just see a mash up and associate anything horned with the Devil.

Research is Key

If you are interested in any type of practice or religion, take the time to research them. You would be amazed at how many belief systems cross into others. Most important, if someone feels or believes in something different from you, let them. Do what you feel is most comfortable for you. There is no way to know what the correct path is, only which one suits you.

Section 2

Occult

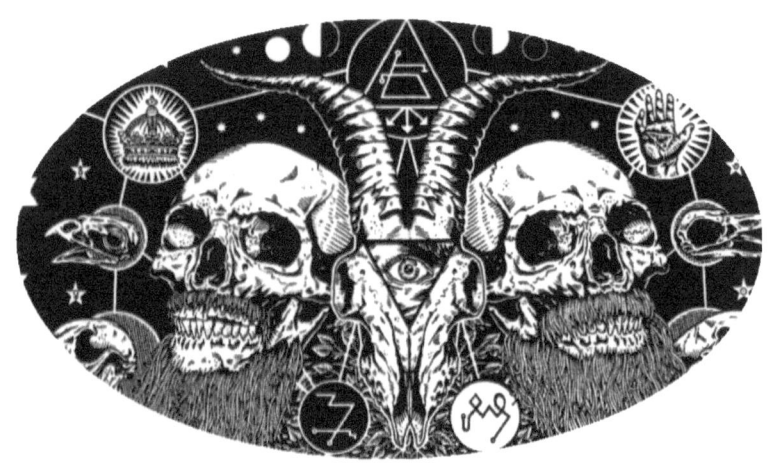

Binding Spells

What is a binding spell?

A binding spell is used for a few reasons. Most commonly, it is used as a form of protection. You are binding or preventing someone from doing harm to you or harm to themselves. Other types of binding spells are used to keep a person, or even at times a spirit, close to you.

Why are binding spells controversial?

A well-known rule in any magical practice explains that you are not allowed to do anything that effects the free will of another being. When you are performing a binding spell, you are preventing that person from certain actions; therefore, you are, in a way, interfering with their free will. However, if their will is to harm you in some way, does that make it acceptable to do this ritual? There are a few things to consider before accessing this loophole.

When is a binding spell acceptable?

Many feel a binding spell should be used as a last resort. There are other options to explore first. One should always begin with trying a protection spell. These can be quite simple or elaborate. These spells are designed to protect you directly from any ill intent. The only time the other person can be affected is with the rule of three. Whatever intent the person attempts to display will return to them with three times the intensity. They get what they give. Protection spells are very personal and there are hundreds of different combinations to research depending on your needs, experience and comfort level. Banishing is another option. Usually banishing spells are used to rid your space or yourself of a negative spirit or type of energy, again this can be as simple or complex as you like. Banishing a person is also frowned upon as manipulative magic just like binding. Attempting to banish a person is, in my opinion, more dangerous than binding. You are not only attempting to stop this person from causing harm, you are attempting to rid yourself of this person completely. There are very few positive outcomes to this situation. Redirecting a person's intent is very different from redirecting the person completely.

How do I perform a binding spell?

There are many ways to perform these spells. One of the simplest ways is to write the person's name on a piece of paper, place it in a zip lock bag and fill with water. Place the bag in the freezer. This is believed to "freeze" the ill intent in its tracks. Forms that are more complex require a poppet or likeness of the person, and a cord, usually black to symbolize reversal and protection. The likeness is then literally bound with the cord. There are also forms of candle magic where the person's name is inscribed onto the candle. Some may use a picture or write down what they are banished from on a piece of paper. You can use colored ink to express your emotion, red for anger, purple for sadness etc. The candle is then lit with the picture or pieces of paper wrapped around with black linen or cotton. The wax will drip, coating everything; these spells are sometimes done for up to a week.

When is binding dangerous?

Preventing harm is one thing but attempting to keep someone from living their life is entirely another. As I previously mentioned, some use binding to keep a person or spirit close to them. In Greek mythology, Deianira gave Hercules a tunic soaked in centaur blood. She believed this could be used as a love potion to keep her husband faithful but the blood was poisoned and burned Hercules. The only time binding in this form is acceptable is during a hand fasting ceremony. This is used as a symbol of two people being bound together. Using different colored cords draped across each other's hands the cords are then tied to symbolize the union. In this case both parties are knowingly involved and in agreement of the ritual. I personally had a hand fasting as part of our wedding. On a more advanced and very dangerous level, binding is used to keep an entity close by to perform the practitioner's bidding. The theory is if you are powerful enough to bind a spirit, you are powerful enough to release it when you are done. This should never be attempted in my opinion. Certain entities, especially non-human, often have their own agenda that will not be to your benefit.

Blood Magic

Blood Magic is one of the most taboo topics in magical practice and beliefs. Though I do not practice this type of magic myself, I'd like to answer some common questions on this topic.

What Is Blood Magic?

Blood magic is the use of the practitioner's own blood, or someone else's, to help personalize and amplify a spell or ritual. Many feel the act of adding blood shows their truest intent and if they are trying to work with a deity, this increases the possibility of cooperation from the deity as well as expediting the desired outcome.

Why Is Blood So Important?

Blood is our life force. We associate blood with death, birth, healing and harming. Blood brings forth strong emotions. Without it, we would cease to exist. We use terms like "flesh and blood" and "blood of Christ' daily. Our blood is the purest part of us.

How Much Blood Is Used?

Just a few drops are recommended. Depending on the practitioner and the spell, there are different techniques. There is the practice for women to use menstrual blood collected during a new or full moon also known as "moon blood". This blood is sometimes used in fertility and love spells. Some feel moon blood works well as an offering to the earth to help plants grow. Blood from pricking your finger can be used in other spells such as protection, health, and for those who choose to practice, curses or revenge spells.

When Is Blood Magic Acceptable?

There is no way to dictate exactly when to perform this type of spell work or ritual, there are some suggestions. If you choose to use blood magic, you must understand this is one of the most intense ways to practice so your requirements must be just as serious. For example, if a coworker or neighbor is annoying you, this is not the time for blood magic. However, if you feel your life is in danger, aside from taking proper legal action, this would be a time for blood magic if you chose to do so. Another example would be if you feel you need a little more money for rent, this is not the time for blood magic, but if you are on the verge of becoming homeless, that is a different and more acceptable circumstance. You can also use blood magic for serious health issues.

Is This Safe?

Those who practice blood magic have rules that they choose to follow. First would be only to use a few drops of your own blood, never use someone else's without their permission. They will just make a small pinprick, no blades, no knife, no deep cutting. Always sanitize the area first, make sure you clean it well after, and use an antibiotic ointment on the wound. Some feel you must never ingest blood or make someone else ingest blood in food or drink. These rules can change depending on the practitioner and what they are putting their intent towards, but these are the safest rules to follow.

How Is the Blood Used?

There are many ways to use blood. You can use it to dress candles, put a drop in a dream pillow or mojo bag, place a drop on a piece of paper before burning or placing a drop directly into the flame. Blood can be placed in a Witch bottle for protection or placed inside a poppet for healing. Some may use a drop of their blood as an offering to a deity or, dare I say, a demon.

Why Is This Practice Frowned Upon?

There are a few reasons blood magic is so taboo. This type of magic brings forth images of human and animal sacrifice as well as the old belief that Witches signed a blood pact with the devil. Certain types of media have helped in making this topic dark and mysterious. There is a misconception that this type of practice is reserved for only those who practice "black magic". As I've stated before any type of magic in the wrong hands can be used to cause harm. Blood is a part of rituals involving sacrifice but these rituals are now rare. Sacrifice does still occur in some cultures, usually animal sacrifices as food and offering. These cultures feel the sacrifice is a gift and will make use of every part provided as a thank you to the creature. However, many feel this part of the practice is wrong since most of us view animals as something to protect; again, different parts of the world practice and believe differently.

Blood magic does not have to be done to be a serious practitioner. This is something optional. You should always be confident and comfortable with however you choose to practice.

Centering, Shielding and Grounding

Without energy, there is no practicing magic. Some of the most important things to learn are how to center yourself to gather your energy, how to protect yourself with your energy, and how to rid yourself of excess energy. These techniques are key to any ritual. Keeping in mind, depending on the type of magic you wish to practice, these techniques may vary, but here are the basics.

Centering Yourself

Learning to center yourself is not just helpful for magical practices but for everyday life. This technique can help to relax and relieve stress. Those who are already familiar with meditation will take to this a little easier but anyone is capable of centering. You must begin in a seated position. When you are just beginning with this technique, you may want to first attempt this at home, somewhere where you are familiar and comfortable. Make sure your cell phone, television, computer and all other distractions are off and put away. Start by closing your eyes, taking deep breaths in and slowly exhaling. Repeat this process until you get a good rhythm going. You can try counting or saying a chant to help in the process of regulating your breathing. Soon this will feel very natural and you can move on to harnessing your energy. Start to rub your hands together until you feel heat between them and slowly move your palms apart. You will feel a difference between your palms; some describe it as an electrical charge, or a pulsating energy. If you don't notice this on the first attempt, simply try again. Eventually you'll be able to move your hands in and out while feeling the energy expand and contract, this means you have gained some control. Imagine that energy expanding until it is all around you, and then you can draw it down into you, wherever you feel comfortable. Some focus on the crown of the head, the heart, or wherever you feel you need the extra help. Soon this will all be second nature and you can do this anywhere, even in a crowd.

Shielding Yourself

Learning to shield yourself is another useful skill. This is a way of protecting yourself from outside energies that can have a negative effect on you. We have all been around certain people who make you feel drained or even weak. You may have heard the term "Energy Vampire", this helps to ensure you are safe from such people, whether they realize what they are putting out or not. Basically, once you've mastered how to control and move your energy you can use it to create a barrier around your entire body. Some visualize a glowing golden orb of positivity, others, a mirror like globe surrounding them. Many believe it is important the shield you create be reflective. This allows additional protection against anyone who is purposefully trying to attack you. Any harmful energy they attempt to send your way will reflect off you.

Grounding Yourself

Once you have finished using the energy you've gathered, whether it be for spell work, healing, or just getting through the day, you need to know how to rid yourself of the excess. How do you know if you have excess energy? You may feel, jittery or shaky, almost like you have taken in too much caffeine, only it's from harnessing your own energy. Grounding is like centering only instead of taking and focusing that energy inward, you are directing it outward. How to release this energy is important, it is not wise just to toss your hands up, releasing it into the air. You must be cautious of any magically inclined people around you who may accidentally absorb your energy. Always know where it is going. Some imagine the energy coursing down through their legs and feet, moving it directly into the ground. If you wish to use something more physical you can direct the energy into a stone, crystal, pot of dirt, a tree, or anything natural that can take on the absorption. Remember, if you are using a stone or crystal, to follow proper cleansing techniques before reusing the same object. You will feel calm and at peace upon proper release of this extra energy.

Common Banishing Techniques

Some people are not very open to the idea of a spirit in their home, especially if the spirit has shown ill or malicious intent. If you wanted to try a banishing on your own, a few common tools are used throughout many cultures and religions. Here are a few ideas.

Technique 1. Ask Politely

The simplest technique is to ask the spirit to leave. Many human entities do not realize their physical bodies have passed. They do not realize what they are doing or their mere presence is frightening. Telling the spirit to move on, giving them permission to leave and telling them, they no longer belong here can work. However, some spirits, especially if you are dealing with a non-human entity, can be more stubborn and therefore more difficult to convince to evacuate your space.

Technique 2. Water

Water, the element that helps sustain life and makes up a huge part of our bodies and our planet, is a readily available tool that can also be used. The key is to have the water blessed by a religious official. This does not mean you must go to a Christian or Catholic, there are officials in every religion that can bless the water and the result will be the same. The water can act as a barrier or a transitory plane. Wet your fingers with the water and mark all entryways into your home.

Technique 3. Sage & Salt

Another common practice is the use of sage. Sage has been used by many cultures and is widely believed to help protect as well as cast out negative energy. Sage sticks are lit then the flame is blown out, allowing the bundle to smolder. Allow the smoke to trail as you walk around the haunted area, it is believed the smoke will capture the negative energy and carry it away as the smoke is fanned out through open windows and doorways.

Salt, preferably sea salt, is crucial to have in any banishing ritual. Salt acts as a barrier that the entity cannot pass. I like to use salt towards the end of a cleansing/banishing ritual as a way of sealing off the area, assuring unwanted spirits cannot return.

Technique 4. Write It Out

We all know the power of the written word. Try writing the problems you have been facing with this spirit on a piece of paper, be as specific as possible, names, dates etc. Follow with writing your intentions. Let the spirit know it is not welcome and you wish to reclaim your space, then proceed to burn the sheet of paper with a candle of your choice. White candles can be used for protection and black candles can be used for banishing. You may want to place the paper in a clean white bowl for a controlled burn. The smoke will carry the negative energy away.

Technique 5. A Frustrating Challenge

Finally, a method that seems to work mainly for non-human entities. These entities can be malicious and very difficult to remove. One theory is that these spirits do not like to be challenged. Taking a small bag of tiny grains, such as sand or rice, place it in the doorways with the contents spilling out. There is a belief that the entity must stop and count every grain. This task is nearly impossible and the entity should grow frustrated at being unable to complete this challenge and will leave your space and move on.

The one thing you must remember when using any of these methods, is you must believe that what are you doing will work and put confidence behind everything you do and say. If you don't stand behind your ritual or allow fear or skepticism to take over, you will not succeed.

Creating a Book of Shadows

What is a Book of Shadows?

A Book of Shadows is a very important tool when it comes to working with any type of magic. This is a book you will use to document all your magical workings and outcomes. You do not have to be a certain type of practitioner; Pagans, Wiccans, Shamans, and Druids all have a way of record keeping.

Book of Shadows vs Grimoire

Many people believe there really is no difference between a Book of Shadows and a Grimoire. Some feel a Book of Shadows is more personal than a Grimoire. A Grimoire is primarily for full spells and rituals, while a Book of Shadows holds all your personal experiences and notes about your magical path.

How to create a Book of Shadows

You don't need a fancy large embroidered book from a local metaphysics shop to start with. One of the most popular ways to create a BOS is with a simple three ring binder. This makes it easy for organization. You'll be able to add, remove and rearrange pages as needed. More importantly, the book you choose to use will need to be consecrated like all your magical tools. You'll need to remove all previous energy and replace it with your own. How you choose to do this is entirely up to you. Each practitioner has their own ritual they like to perform.

Another common question is if a BOS can be digital. In these modern times, this may be an easier method and that's fine. However, it is believed that writing your own BOS by hand helps with transferring your energy into the book. Some practitioners choose to write in a magical alphabet. Unless you are completely fluent in these alphabets, this is believed not to be very practical when you need to reference something quickly. Whichever way you decide to document, be sure to have a title page, your name, date and a page to write a blessing for your book, this can also be a dedication to a certain deity if you prefer. If you are part of a coven, you may need to copy your initiation ceremony here as well.

What Should I Put in My Book of Shadows?

Every practitioner's BOS is different, as they should be. There is no right or wrong way to construct this tool. There are a few common suggestions. The Wheel of The Year is something to use to track Sabbats, celebrations, and festivals you acknowledge. A list of deities, Gods and Goddesses you honor and work with in spell casting and your personal notes on each. You may also want to keep a table of moon phases, color meanings, uses for crystals and herbs as well as their healing properties. If you practice divination, you can keep a list and diagrams of tarot spreads, scrying sessions, or pendulum work. For the kitchen Witch, be sure to write down all your recipes and magical ingredients. When you are feeling crafty make notes and even drawings of any poppet, dream pillow, magical soap or candle you create. Include what you used to create it, what purpose it will serve and what the outcome was once it was utilized. Another important section to create is a dream and meditation journal, you can be as detailed as you like. Keep note of any symbols or themes that are recurring. Many practitioners also keep a list of books they have read and studied in the magical arts and how they have helped in their journey. Finally, spells; document your spell work, how you prepared, how you performed, how you closed, and the outcome. Did the spell work or do you feel you need to adjust it a bit? Anything and everything to do with your craft goes in these pages. Therefore, a three-ring binder is useful. You can create sections, used colored tabs and be as organized as you like for easy and quick reference.

Is there anything you shouldn't put in a Book of Shadows?

There are a few rules when creating and managing your BOS. Of course, this isn't the place for dear diary I had a bad day, if it isn't part of your spiritual path, it doesn't go in the book. Never write anything with the intent of ill will or harm to yourself or another, no curses, no hexes or hateful speech. Remember this is your book; no one else besides yourself should be writing in it or using your Book. Each person's relationship with the magical arts is very different so no two Books of Shadows will be the same.

Creating Your Own Magic

The power that lies within all of us is remarkable to say the least. For centuries, the capabilities of the human mind have been an intriguing mystery. Everyone and everything around us contains an energy. The ability to change or manipulate that energy is what spell work is all about.

Rules and Guidelines

There are guidelines to spells and rituals that must be followed. One simply cannot grab a spell book and start crafting. Before beginning to perform magic, you must first have a complete understanding of yourself, your current mental state, and your intentions. For example, grabbing a book of revenge spells from your local bookstore because you are angry with someone is not the correct way to go about things. Always remember The Rule of Three: What you release out will return. Many do not even realize how powerful ill intentions can be, until it is too late. I have had many people state that they feel the rule of three is just for Wiccans; I do not believe this to be true. Karma is everywhere. I have always believed that magic is neither black nor white; it is all in the intent of the practitioner. Now that we've covered a few basic rules, here are a few brief guidelines in crafting your own spells.

Tools and Supplies

Once you've decided what the intent of your spell is going to be, you'll need to gather some supplies. Keep in mind magic relies heavily on symbolism; color, texture, material, and even scents will have a direct impact. Decide if you'll be using candles; if so, what color? Black is often used for protection, white for purification, blue for serenity, and so on. Certain herbs can also be used: rosemary to promote pleasant dreams, thyme for peace of mind, or bay leaves to help protect against the magic of others. Carefully consider every detail, including what type of ink and paper you'll be using. Many practitioners make their own ink. Dragon's blood, dove's blood, raven's blood, and butterfly blood are all common names of "magical inks." These inks of course are not made with actual blood, simply creative names given due to the color they produce. There are even recipes to make your own disappearing ink if you wish to keep your work completely private. Those that make their own ink will also use the creative opportunity to make their own quill; this helps to bring a more natural element to the project. Another thing to think about is the types of paper. Many have their own book of shadows, some use parchment, and others keep index cards. These are all just suggestions, of course; this can be as simple or complex as you wish. A pen and notepad from an office supply will also work. Remember, it is the energy you put forth that will make or break the spell.

Writing the Words

A common question is whether these spells can be written using a computer. This technique is usually not recommended because it lacks a certain personal aspect. Pen to paper generates more energy and therefore keeps the process closer to the "old ways." However, do what makes you comfortable and gives you the best energy. When writing the spell, think about the structure. Are you going to call upon the help of a deity, and if so what role do they play to carry out your intent? Keep in mind that calling upon and evocation is highly advanced and can be dangerous to even a seasoned practitioner. The spell should contain an opening, stating your intent, a body (containing the actual spell or ritual), and a closing (when the spell is to be completed). Don't forget to thank the deity you've called upon if you chose to do so. Closing a spell is very important. This ensures the release of your intent and closes any spiritual barriers, if opened. Many spells are written in poetic verse; this creates a type of rhythm and may help in the visualization of the flow of energy. This does not have to be the only method. This is the most personal part of the process and can be written however you feel comfortable. Try not to get too complicated at first. Memorizing your words is usually best, so keep it simple.

Timing Is Everything

It is advisable to research when the best time would be to carry out your spell work. Moon phase, astrological place, time of day, month, and day of the week all play a very important part in magic. For example, a new moon on a Monday would be best for a healing spell, since both represent purity and new beginnings. There are numerous combinations to research and consider, so it can be overwhelming at first. These things take practice. The more you learn, the easier it will become.

Working Your Magic

Now you are ready to perform your magic. Make sure you are in a private space where you will not be disturbed. You do not need an alter but if you already have one, even better. Prepare yourself and your environment. Take a cleansing bath or drink a calming tea. Ground yourself using your favorite meditation technique. If you need to cast a circle or call the quarters, do so before the actual spell is to begin. When starting your work, make sure your intent is clear. Speak with confidence. If you do not believe in what you are saying, then stop here. A spell carried out with doubt or fear, will not work at all or it could potentially backfire. Once your spell is finished, be sure to complete every step, such as allowing the candle to burn out on its own and burying or burning certain items that aid in carrying the energy and intent of your spell. Remain safe: Do not burn anything that cannot be a controlled burn, and do not destroy or trespass on someone else's property to bury an object. The common rule is to wait a Lunar month, or about 28 days, to see if your spell was successful. You may need to repeat your process or make some changes if needed. Finally, NEVER use magic to attempt to change the free will of another. Spell work that involves another person without their knowledge is dangerous and goes against the moral standards of any good practitioner in my opinion.

Dowsing / Divining & Pendulum Work

Dowsing and Divining

The use of dowsing or divining tools have been utilized in science, medicine and even magic for centuries; it seems to be one of the most universal tools used. Pendulums, rods and sticks play a part in this technique which is basically a way to find hidden things. You may be familiar with dowsing rods that are used to locate water, metal, oil, and have even been used as a technique in ghost hunting. Many believe the term dowsing is defined as searching for a specific physical item and the term divining is defined as searching for specific information.

A Brief History

The use of dowsing is believed to go back at least eight thousand years according to wall murals and artwork from China, Egypt and North Africa. During the 15th Century, those who used this technique were thought to be practitioners of evil. This is believed to be the origin of another term used for dowsing called "water Witching". The practice did not go away however and has been continually used to this day for many different purposes. Marines in the Vietnam War used dowsing to help locate hidden mines and underground tunnels. Doctors in France have used pendulums to help diagnose illness and many may have witnessed the use of this tool to determine the sex of an unborn child. Today those who use this technique are called practitioners of Radiesthesia.

How Does It Work?

So how does it work? The most common theory is that it's all about energy. Everything and everyone in the world gives off some sort of energy. Certain energies are drawn to each other. Water gives off incredible energy therefore dowsing for water has worked and continues to work very well. The material used in the dowsing tool can vary. Some are made of metal or a forked wooden stick, and pendulums can be almost anything, stone, crystal, and even a pocket watch. When the tool meets a certain energy, it will respond. Dowsing rods will cross each other, pendulums will swing back and forth or in circular motions and the simple forked wooden stick will direct you as you walk with it in your hands. However, there is another theory that the tool responds to your own subconscious and is therefore an extension of the "psychic" mind; this brings me to how this is used as a divining tool.

Divination Technique

Many who practice modern magic have used pendulums as divination tools. They are believed to help find answers to questions and even read the energy off an object. Therefore, if you plan to use this technique you first have to choose your pendulum. As I previously mentioned, a pendulum can be anything that is a small weight attached to a piece of thread or chain. You will come across many colors, materials and shapes. The best advice for choosing one is simply go with your gut. When you first start to work with a pendulum you need to test its response with you. I personally follow the standard technique of placing your elbow on the table and holding the string of the pendulum between the forefinger and thumb. Make sure you are steady and the pendulum can move freely. Now say "Give me a yes" and watch which position it begins to move, left to right or back and forth. You may need to repeat the question to get a definite answer. Continue by saying "Give me a no" and watch how the pendulum moves, hopefully in the opposite direction of the first response. Once you are confident with how the pendulum will move with yes or no questions you may want to ask something that you know the answer to as a test of the accuracy of the tool. When an answer is unclear, the pendulum may move in an uneven pattern. To utilize the technique of reading the energy off an object simply hold the pendulum over the object in question. The pendulum may begin to move slowly or rapidly depending upon the amount of energy; if the motion is clockwise, you are dealing with a positive energy, counter clockwise means a negative energy. Finally, the wider the circle created by the pendulum, the stronger the energy.

Dream Magic

Dreaming is a topic that always seems to spark the interest of many. There are thousands of resources regarding dream interpretation and dream symbol meaning. There are even common dream symbols, such as falling, being chased or losing teeth that many people have. Many do not realize that magic can play just as big of a part in our sleeping life as our waking life. With some effort and the right combination of items, we can use magic to assist us in this dream realm.

Induce Lucid Dreaming

This is a topic I won't spend too long discussing because it has been covered so many times by so many great authors and teachers. Lucid dreaming is a state in which you are aware you are dreaming and can therefore gain control of yourself or even your environment and adjust things to your liking. Lucid dreaming really isn't considered a form of magic; however, there are a few magical rituals one can try to help increase their chances of having a lucid dream. Many practitioners believe that Mugwort is a key ingredient in the practice of dream magic. You can try drinking a Mugwort tea, taking a warm bath with a few drops of Mugwort oil or even add it into a dream pillow that you can easily make yourself.

Dream Pillows

A dream pillow is a small pillow you can either buy or make yourself. You fill the pillow with herbs and oils depending on your needs. They have many uses such as comfort, healing, and protection just to name a few. They do not have to be utilized just for dreaming, you can also keep one with you during travel, a stressful job interview or a scary hospital stay. What you put into the pillow is very personal, so I suggest you do your research to fit your needs. Scent can trigger some very powerful emotions and memories.

Dreaming of the Future

Having prophetic dreams seems like a good idea, gazing into your future as you slumber. Some of the most common ways this is believed to be achieved is with the use of Jasmine and Damiana, both are believed to induce psychic ability as well as increase the energy given to a spell or ritual. The Jasmine is usually sprinkled on or around the pillow while some choose to burn the Jasmine instead. Burning Jasmine seems to be one of the keys to bringing prophetic dreams since it is known to be associated with the moon and night in general. Damiana is believed to be added in for the more specific request of revealing your true loves or passions in life.

No More Nightmares

There are a few common techniques to help with nightmares. One is the use of the Anise seed. For centuries, this seed is believed to help in warding off the evil eye and for general protection. You can place the seed in a dream pillow or carry it with you in a white mojo bag. Another way is to light a white candle and tie a silver ribbon around it, place the candle in front of you and meditate while staring into the flame. Once you are relaxed, take the candle and look to the moon. Now, you will speak to the moon and stars asking for peace, protection, and to be surrounded by beauty. The words you speak are of your own choosing; just make sure your intentions are clear. Once you are done, extinguish the flame and tie the silver ribbon around your wrist. Peaceful sleep shall follow.

Dream a Little Dream of Me

There are spells to make someone dream of you, do I recommend you try them? The short answer is no. Magic must never be used to manipulate another person. You must never use magic on someone who is not aware you are doing so. The only time this would be acceptable is if you really wanted to try this type of spell and you asked someone to be a willing participant. The same is true for spells that claim they will help you dream of the deceased. We all have someone we miss and would love to see again. If a deceased loved one wishes to make an appearance, it should be their will, not ours. Calling forth the deceased is a dangerous practice, there are always multiple spirits wanting to come through and communicate. Whom you bring through may not be whom you intended, so please let them choose when and how they visit.

Every Day Magic

Many people in this world practice Witchcraft and other forms of the magical arts. However, there are also many people who don't. Even if you do not consider yourself a magical practitioner or are even slightly skeptical, several things you may do daily qualify as a type of magic. Whether you are avoiding bad luck or trying to ensure safety from unseen forces. Here are a few of them.

Unlucky Thirteen

Many avoid this number without questioning why. There are a few different theories. In Christianity, it is believed that Judas, betrayer of Jesus, was the thirteenth guest during the last supper. In similar Norse legend, the thirteenth guest was Loki who killed one of the other Gods, initiating a chain reaction of destruction. In Japan, the unlucky number is four because it closely resembles the word "shi" for death.

Spilling Salt

Why do we toss salt over our shoulders if we spill a little? Again, we visit the story of the last supper. Leonardo da Vinci's painting shows that Judas had knocked over the salt with his elbow. This is a symbol of treachery and lies. Salt is also credited with the ability to offer a protective barrier, keeping any evil at bay. Tossing salt over your shoulder, left shoulder to be exact was also believed to blind any evil entities lurking near you.

Walking Under Ladders

There are a couple of origin stories behind this one. First in Medieval times, it was thought the ladder resembled the gallows and walking underneath it was thought to bring your own death by hanging. A couple more theories revolve around the shape the ladder makes while it's leaning against the wall, a triangle. For the ancient Egyptians, the power of the pyramid was crucial and walking through this triangle was breaking the power. In Christianity, this shape resembles the Holy Trinity, walking through is considered desecration and an invitation to the Devil.

Blowing Out Birthday Candles

Almost everyone does this on their birthday and you have to get them all or your wish won't come true. Do we know why? Some believe this began in ancient Greece. People would bring cakes with candles to Artemis, goddess of the hunt. The candles represented the glowing of the moon. Germans used birthday cakes with candles in the 1700s during a festival for children. The candle represented the light of life. Finally, many cultures believe smoke carries our prayers and wishes to the heavens where they will be heard and they hoped answered.

Knocking on Wood

I do this one often. You say something hopeful and promising, and then you immediately knock on the nearest piece of wood, but why? This dates to the Pagan belief of nature spirits. Many beings were believed to live in the trees, some to help and some to harm. Knocking on wood today is a way to chase off any entities who have evil intent once hearing your plan of good fortune. Another theory suggests that it is a way of requesting aide from a helpful entity to carry out your wish.

Bless You

Yet another superstition with a few origin stories; one is that Pope Gregory the Great said 'God Bless You" to people who sneezed during the bubonic plague, another is the belief that sneezing allows your soul to leave your body as well as the brief stoppage of your heart. Saying 'Bless You" welcomes you back to life.

Umbrella Indoors

One common theory about why opening an umbrella indoors is bad luck dates to the Egyptian era, umbrellas were used as protection from the sun. Opening one indoors was a direct insult to the Sun God Ra. There is also the belief that the umbrella was made to resemble the Goddess Nut who created the sky. The shade of the umbrella was considered, as a symbol of her image, sacred and only allowed for royalty; any non-royal person under the umbrella was believed to have bad luck follow them due to their sacrilege.

Evocation vs Invocation

What's the Difference?

The words Evoke and Invoke are sometimes used interchangeably but they are two very different things. The one thing they do have in common is they are both extremely advanced and dangerous forms of magic. One simply cannot call upon an entity blindly. Both techniques require years of practice and knowledge.

What does it mean to Evoke?

This is when you call upon an entity to join you. This entity can help you complete your spell work by working with you. Depending on your belief or type of magic, who this entity is can greatly vary. There are numerous rituals to evoke different entities; however, the risk is great. When asking this entity to join you, they may not respond, they may not be pleased with the offerings you've brought. Depending on the spell and whom you are evoking, these offerings could be a certain type of flower, fruit, or material like wood or burlap. Some entities require "darker" offerings and these are especially risky. There may be many attempts made before you evoke a spirit successfully. When you have finally succeeded you may see them in your mind's eye, or you will feel a shift or a change in the air around you. Evocation usually works best within a controlled circle and with multiple participants. These spirits may be open to coming into our plane but not very open to being controlled by a human. One should never attempt to do this alone. Proper opening and closing of the circle is also very crucial. You never want these spirits left alone; they can and will cause mischief. Always be sure to dismiss them back to where they came from in an assertive and no-nonsense matter.

What does it mean to Invoke?

This is when you call upon an entity to work within you, usually the higher deities, Gods and Goddesses. When you invoke, you are literally opening yourself up to voluntary possession. This allows you to perform your spell work with the ultimate use of energy and power. Once again, depending upon the type of magic you are practicing, whom you invite in will differ, as well as what heightened abilities you'll possess. You may have increased clairvoyance or gain the ability to speak to the deceased. When you invoke you are taking a huge risk. Some practitioners feel, depending on the deity, you may not have control over your physical body. There have been reports of people who invoke experiencing time lapses and memory loss. Others suggest you will have control over your body but you must release the deity and all heightened abilities quickly. Holding onto the energy for an extended amount of time is extremely dangerous and may result in physical and mental harm.

Invoke to Evoke?

A common theory states that in order to evoke properly, you must first invoke. Usually the deities you invoke within you are more powerful than the spirits you evoke to assist you. Therefore, the spirits you evoke are more likely to listen and cooperate if you have a higher power within you. Unfortunately, when invocation is on the table too many people turn to Demonic entities. People feel that since demons are feared they are the most powerful and the results will come more efficiently. Demons are very powerful indeed but they are never to be trusted. Even with years of research and study, even if you feel you have formed a bond, they always want something in return, the bigger the request, the bigger the sacrifice. Many people who attempt to invoke any deity are not prepared and have horrible and traumatic experiences.

Is spirit summoning ever a good idea?

Practitioners have their own path and individual goals to reach. I suggest anyone interested in this form of magic do their research, listen to experience, and then do a little more research. This is magic, not a game.

Love/Hate Magic

There are so many books and articles available on magic and how to use magic to make your life better. One important point I see few practitioners make is that magic is not meant to work for you; it is meant to work with you. Spell casting, channeling, divination, and all other forms of magic are meant to be an extension of your energy, your intentions, and your will, not something to perform randomly. True magic takes time. Gathering and grounding your own energy is something that must be mastered first or your attempts will be unsuccessful. Magic is nothing to play with or take lightly.

I Want to Use Magic to Help Me Find My True Love

I have come across many "love spells," and honestly, it saddens me. I have also had the misfortune of seeing some websites offering to help cast these spells, for a fee of course. This is when it is important to understand what is acceptable and completely unacceptable when it comes to spell casting. One of the first rules to follow is never, under any circumstances, perform any type of magic involving another human being without their permission. You cannot force someone to feel a certain way. You should not attempt to manipulate their free will for any reason. Many "spells" make false promises that you'll be able to make someone dream of you or even make someone obsess over you. There is no explanation needed for how severely that could backfire. Glamour spells are also popular, offering the ability to make you appear beautiful and desirable. That is something you need to project on your own.

So, What is an Acceptable Way to Use Magic for Love?

Focus on spells that aim toward self-empowerment, confidence boosting, and improving social skills. These are all things that will help you present your best true self, and the appropriate people will be attracted to your new energy.

Someone Has Really Hurt Me. I Want Revenge! How About a Curse?

A few years ago, I was offered a writing gig for a book on revenge spells and curses. I respectfully declined. This, in my opinion, is the absolute worst way to go about mending your hurt. I'd like to talk about another common rule in magic, the Rule of Three. Whatever energy you put out will return to you threefold. Of course, there are going to be plenty of revenge spells and curses available for the willing "spell caster" to perform, for a fee of course. Magic should never be used to cause harm to another, ever. It doesn't matter how deep the hurt is. The repercussions will be three times as severe. Spells that promise to give someone bad luck, nightmares, or even curse them are to be avoided at all cost, pun intended. I've seen directions on how to cast curses just like the Ancient Egyptians used and some claiming to be passed down from Gypsy culture. Regardless of how you dress it in pretty labels, negative energy is all the same and it is nothing to tamper with.

So, Is There an Acceptable Way to Use Magic to Get Revenge?

Once again, in my opinion, no, there is no acceptable way to use magic to get revenge. However, you can learn the power of a good protection spell to aid in combatting the negative energy of others, especially the ones who hurt you. There are also spells that assist in communication to avoid future misunderstandings. In addition, anti-anxiety and anti-depression spells work very well and will help you gain knowledge into what you do and do not want in your life for future happiness.

How Do I Know What Spells Are Acceptable to Use?

Consider spells that will help the energy you already possess. Pay attention to the tools you'll need. Natural oils, stones, candles, and items that you hold dear are common and safe. Make sure the spell does not require you to trespass or destroy someone else's property. Avoid anything that suggests harm or ill intent, and never take anything from another person, such as clothing, hair, or nail clippings, without their consent. Spells that promise instant results should also be avoided; remember, magic takes time and dedication. Use caution when you come across someone offering to perform magic for a price. It may cost more than you could ever imagine. The best tool you can use as a practitioner is your own inner voice. If what you're doing seems wrong or nags at your subconscious, then you should step back, assess your intent, and start again.

Necromancy, what is it really?

Necromancy is known as the art is communicating, and even raising, the dead. This controversial type of magic has roots in ancient Egypt, Greece, and Rome. So, what is it, do people really practice necromancy in modern times and why?

Communicating with the dead

When we think of Necromancy our minds jump to digging through graveyards and moving corpses; while this does happen with certain aspects of this type of magic there is more to it, a lot more. The main purpose of necromancy is usually to gain knowledge. Those in the spirit realm are believed to have the ability to see and know all. Some want to know about the afterlife, some want to know if a loved one is finally at peace and some want help in the realm of the living. More common forms of necromancy occur almost daily. Spirit mediums can be considered to be using a form of necromancy when communicating with, or even invoking, spirits. You can also practice a type of this magic with the use of the Ouija board, attempting to seek answers from the spirit world. Other forms of divination, like scrying and certain ancestor spells, can also be considered forms of necromancy. There is a common suggestion for anyone attempting to try this form of magic: they should start with trying to communicate with family members. This way the practitioner can more easily gauge how the spirit is going to react and it will more than likely be a friendly one to work with.

Raising the dead

This type of Necromancy, where you are literally attempting to raise the dead, is considered one of the darkest forms of magic. Usually the practitioner is looking for something for personal gain such as the location of hidden treasures, sacred knowledge or even how to best conjure and control another spirit. They are willing to do whatever it takes to obtain this information. These rituals have been attempted for centuries and the steps have not changed much over the years. There is a belief that it is easier to raise a body that has been deceased less than a year. They are more likely to be near their burial place. The older the corpse, the more difficult it is to raise. Necromancers would use many different locations such as underground vaults, forests, churches, and graveyards. Crossroads were also popular locations. Anywhere the practitioner would not be disturbed would do.

There were nine days of preparation before the ritual. Necromancers would dress themselves in clothes taken from a corpse while reciting their own funeral rites. These clothes were to remain on until the ritual was complete. The food they ate could not contain salt, since salt is a preservative. They ate black unleavened bread and drank unfermented grape juice. The only meat they could eat was dog meat since dogs were a symbol of the goddess Hecate. The basic idea was to surround themselves with death. When it was time for the ritual the necromancer would go to their location between midnight and 1 am. A circle would be drawn around the grave. Saffron, wood and mandrake would be burning as they exhumed the body. Soon the body would be place with its head facing the East, towards the rising sun, and the arms would be outstretched. A bowl of wine and sweet oil would be placed near the right hand of the corpse as an offering. Soon the necromancer would touch the corpse three times with their wand while reciting their incantations. Now it was believed the spirit of the deceased would enter the body and it would slowly rise.

The practitioner would begin by asking questions and the spirit would respond in a low voice. Once the necromancer was satisfied with the answers they had received, they would release the spirit and would either burn the body or bury it in quicklime to dissolve it so no one else could force it to rise again.

Is Necromancy Dangerous?

The short answer, in my opinion, is yes. This type of magic is considered to be very difficult to preform and very dangerous. Usually spirits are not happy about being called back into their old body. Spirits can become confused and at times angry and violent. Some necromancers go beyond wanting to raise the dead and attempt to raise and control other non-human spirits such as demons or elementals. Usually their purpose is to use these beings to carry out attacks on whomever they wish to cause harm and suffering. Another reason this is a risky type of magic is the theory that these spirts can attempt to drain the practitioner of their own life force. These spirits are looking for another body and yours can be quite tempting to them. Finally, disturbing a grave is both illegal and morally wrong. Leave the dead where they lay and focus on the power you contain within your own living, breathing self.

Poppet Magic

What Is Poppet Magic?

Poppets are used in a type of spell work called sympathetic magic. The belief behind sympathetic magic is that you can affect a person by preforming magical workings on something that represents them. A poppet is a figure that represents a person or animal you wish to help, or heal, with magic.

Isn't a Poppet Just a Voodoo Doll?

Popular modern movies and television programs have done their part in portraying the use of poppets as "voodoo dolls", fanning the flames of fear and misinformation with this type of magic. The use of these dolls goes back much further than the roots of Voodoo. In fact, these dolls aren't really used in true Haitian Vodou at all. Poppets can be traced as far back as ancient Egypt when several enemies of Ramses III used wax figures representing him to aid in causing his demise. In ancient Greece, these dolls were used to bind lovers together or to keep a spirit from causing harm. This concept is similar to West African Fetish magic imported by slaves coming into America bringing these dolls, called fetishes, with them. A fetish was believed to contain spirits connected to the person who owned the doll and it would be worn as a talisman. Poppets are also used in Hoodoo, which is a type of folk magic not to be confused with the religion of Voodoo. Though "voodoo dolls" are popular in New Orleans, it is mainly a way to appease tourists.

How Do You Make a Poppet?

There are many ways to make a poppet. You can use cloth, wax, wood, clay, or even meat. If you are making one from fabric, you can use cotton or other bits of cloth or polyfill to stuff the doll but be sure to leave room for the magic. Keep in mind your purpose for creating the doll, use whichever herbs or stones that will help fuel your magical workings, and don't forget your taglock. A taglock is the key item that will connect the poppet to whomever it is intended for. This can be hair, nail clippings, clothing, photographs, or anything else to create a strong link. These can go inside or outside of the doll. Remember to incorporate colors that will help show your intent, black for banishing, white for protection, blue for healing, orange for creativity and so on. Make the poppet appear as similar as possible to whomever it will be linked. Make sure to have arms, legs, head, and torso. Keep in mind if this person has any tattoos, scars, or other distinguishing features that should be added to the doll for proper representation. You can draw, paint or etch a face, add any signs or symbols, especially astrological, keeping in mind that the more you put into it the more powerful it is believed to be. You are encouraged to speak during the preparations, speaking your intent and giving the doll its purpose. Poppets can also be made for animals as well; you'll just have to tweak the shape a bit.

Can Poppets Be Harmful?

Any type of magic in the wrong hands can be harmful. Poppets are meant to represent a being, so the thought of manipulating someone to your will is scary. The purpose is to help and heal. With any form of magic, the person should be aware that these workings are being performed with them in mind. Personally, I do not believe in using poppet magic for love or material gain. For example, you can make a poppet of yourself using a piece of sexy lingerie to help boost your confidence which will help you find love in the long run but you should not make a poppet resembling a person you wish would fall in love with you, especially without them knowing. You can also use your own poppet to help get a job or further your career but do not make a poppet of your boss to try to get a raise. These dolls work great as healing magic for a sick friend, family member or pet. They also come in handy if you need a little extra protection or wish to banish any harm or gossip that may come your way.

Take the Fear Out

Poppets are a fun, creative project you can use in your magical workings. Try to push aside all the misconceptions that have come with these dolls over the centuries and see them for what they are, a tool just like a dream pillow or protective amulet. Your intent is the key, magic should never be used for harm, remember whatever you put forth will be returned to you.

Scrying

Scrying, from the Old English word descry, meaning to "reveal" or "make out dimly," is a form of divination that has been utilized for centuries. This practice was, and still is, used to look into the past, get a glimpse into the future, and even as a way to get messages or warnings about the present. Seers would also use this technique to find lost objects or people, make spiritual journeys, and communicate with the deceased. The Celts, Egyptians, Greeks, and Native Americans all used scrying in different forms. The Greeks and Celts used crystals, water, black glass, and polished quartz. The Egyptians used water or basins filled with oil; they even had techniques for dream scrying, and the Native Americans used smoke to obtain answers from the astral plane.

Mirror, Mirror, on the Wall...

Even in popular culture, we all remember the Evil Queen consulting her magic mirror in Snow White. In more recent works, the use of the Pensieve in the Harry Potter series to "view memories" and learn from the past. Finally, let's not forget how the Wicked Witch was able to keep an eye on Dorothy during her travels down the Yellow Brick Road. When we think of the more modern version of this technique, we think of the beautiful gypsy woman and her crystal ball, but many of us have done some sort of scrying without even recognizing it as such. Cloud gazing is a less recognized form of this type of divination. Think about it; you're lying on the cool grass, relaxed, mind not particularly focused on anything, and suddenly the clouds drifting by start taking shape. Without even realizing it, you've tapped into an ancient form of divination.

Methods of Scrying

The techniques and materials used are vast. Here are just a few examples. The best recognized is crystal gazing, usually with a crystal ball. It is recommended to use natural crystal with imperfections for the best results. Lampadomancy uses the flame from a candle or an oil lamp. The seer looks for messages in the actual flame or the shadows it casts. Another use of candles requires those seeking answers to place three candles in a triangle. If one of the flames burns higher than the other two, this is a positive answer. If the flames are all uneven, danger is near. Flickering flames indicate a journey must be taken, and if the flames are suddenly extinguished, bad luck is inevitable. There is a belief that spirits are attracted to natural elements like fire and water, therefore making it easier to communicate. Ceroscopy is a technique using a pot of melted wax. The wax would be dripped from the pot into cool water, and the wax would then begin to form shapes that would then be interpreted. Hydromancy involves just the water itself, how it flows, what color it is, and how it ripples if a pebble is dropped into it. Some toss a stone into still water and listen to the sound it makes. Mirror gazing is another widely recognized and slightly controversial technique. This requires one to stare, not into, but through the mirror until images begin to form. There are special black mirrors made specifically for scrying. The controversy lies within the superstitions and folklore surrounding mirrors. In the early 20th century, it was believed that if a young woman looked into a hand mirror while walking backwards up a flight of stairs, she would see her future husband. In a less light-hearted legend, it was recommended to cover all the mirrors in a room where a person has died to assure their spirit is not trapped.

Does Scrying Leave You Vulnerable to Spirit Attacks?

Mirrors and other scrying methods have long been believed to be portals for the dead, including the malevolent. When you are performing any form of divination, you must be relaxed, meditative, and open to receive the messages that are to come. Some, including myself, believe that this may leave you vulnerable to the spirit world and more susceptible to troublesome entities. So, the next time you're staring up at the sky or watching shadows dance on the wall, take a moment to think about what these seemingly meaningless shapes may look like. Realize that many centuries ago, people looked to this technique to make important, sometimes life changing decisions. Something more to ponder: Does this form of "fortune telling" rely solely on the subconscious mind? In other words, did people see what they wanted to see and then make decisions based on what they subconsciously already knew? On the other hand, was there really something more magical in the works? Could greater forces beyond our control have a contribution in this ancient art form?

Simple Candle Magic

Candles represent so many things — passion, love, hope, strength, and desire. We have used candles to celebrate, worship and mourn for centuries. Using candles for spell work is very common and one of the easiest forms of magic. The tools required are very simple, but the results can be very powerful. Candles represent the fire element, and this is one of the most direct ways to deliver your intent.

What Kind of Candle Do I Use?

One of the most important things to remember when working with candles for spell work is it must completely burn down on its own. Large and oddly shaped candles are not recommended and can be counterproductive. The standard stick shape is preferred and should be about four to six inches in length. Many metaphysical shops sell "spell candles," and these are fine. Make sure to submerge the candle in sea salt before use, this will help to cleanse it of any previous energy it may have absorbed before you brought it home. Candles made of beeswax are popular because it comes straight from nature. Another option is to make your own candle; in fact, some practitioners prefer this method to all others. Do not, under any circumstances, use a candle that has been previously burned.

Does the Color of the Candle Really Matter?

The color of the candle is going to represent the root of your intent, so do your research. Some common colors include • Red for passion, strength, or courage. Pink for romance and affection. Black for protection and banishing. White for new beginnings and peace. Purple to heighten psychic ability or gain wealth. Blue for protection, inspiration, and devotion. Green for fertility, luck, and abundance. Yellow for imagination and creativity. Orange for attraction, control, and ambition. These are just a few examples. There are many variations of these colors, and every single one has multiple meanings, so choose carefully.

Dressing the Candle: What Does This Mean?

Once the candle has been chosen and cleansed, it is time to dress the candle. This ensures the candle is "charged" with your energy. Dressing the candle requires the use of a few drops of oil. What type of oil you use can vary depending on the spell. You should use an all-natural oil; some prefer grape seed, olive, or lotus. The most important part of this practice is the direction in which the candle is dressed. If your intent is to bring something to you, dress the candle by placing the oil at the top and bring it down toward the middle. Repeat the process with the bottom of the candle, bringing it up toward the middle. If your intent is to repel something from you, start in the middle, bring the oil up toward the top, and then again from the middle, dress it down toward the bottom. Never go back and forth. To give your spell an extra boost, you can also incorporate some herbs that pertain to your intent.

Making Magic

Once the candle is ready, make sure it is lit in a place that is safe. Remember it must burn down completely on its own, so make sure it is somewhere free from drafts. Write your intent on a piece of paper. The paper doesn't have to match the color of your candle, but some will use colored paper to help with the delivery. Once you have written your wish — be as specific as possible — begin folding it slowly. Concentrate intently on what you want and why it is so important to you. Place the edge of the folded paper into the flame until it begins to burn. Hold on as long as you can without burning your fingers, and then place the paper in a fire safe bowl or cauldron, letting it burn completely away. Once your candle has burned completely down, some practitioners will bury the remnants. Many times the process has to be repeated, so do not be disappointed if you don't see immediate results. Magic takes time, and the efforts you put forth will be returned to you.

The Magic of Animals

While getting into my car the other day, I happened to look up to see a hawk perched upon the light post. I knew this beautiful bird was there for a reason. Something was telling me I needed to step back, observe the bigger picture, and redirect my focus. How did I gather this information? As a practitioner, I'm very open to recognizing the signs and symbols that nature will sometimes offer.

Spirit Animal, Totem, & Familiar, What's the Difference?

You may have heard at least one of these terms but are not sure of the differences. First, let's start with the term Spirit Animal. I think a common misconception is a spirit animal is one you choose. This is not the case. A spirit animal will make itself known to you during a time when you need guidance, clarity, or when there is a lesson you must learn. These animals may appear in many ways. You may see the physical animal more often than you have in the past, or you may see artwork, photos, or television ads with this animal. For example, if you are seeing more spiders lately, you may need to focus on a pattern you are creating in your life. Another example to consider is noticing animals that you may not see in your daily life. You may not live in an area where goats are prevalent but you're suddenly seeing images of them everywhere. You're noticing artwork or television ads with a goat as the star, or you may be dreaming of goats and this is not usual for you. These animals are a sign that you are sure of your current path and are reaching new heights. Try not to let your personal feeling of the animal interfere with the message it is attempting to bring.

You may think frogs are slimy and gross but they are a symbol of healing and hidden beauty.

A totem is an animal that is called upon to help with a task or offer guidance and protection. Many tribes use animal totems to tell the story of their heritage and ancestors. These totems are believed to have special powers that help the tribe carry out certain duties. The word Totem is from the Chippewa word for kinship group. Some examples of totems are the bear that symbolizes solitude and strength. The Coyote is there to help you recognize when you've made a mistake and the Deer shows kindness and compassion. These symbols are very important and even the smallest creatures can be extremely powerful.

A familiar is referred to usually in magical practices such as Shamanism and Witchcraft. During the European Witch hunts and Salem Witch trials, these creatures were believed to be given to Witches as a gift from Satan. Unfortunately, this led to many domestic animals being killed during this time. Back to the modern day, a familiar is believed to be a connection between this world and the unseen realms. Possibly, because animals have been known to see and hear things we cannot. A common belief is that a familiar will find you, like when a stray cat or dog randomly arrives at your door. There are also meditation techniques to help visualize and even summon your familiar.

Animals "In" Magic (Literally)

Yes, people have and still do use actual animal parts in magical practices. In Shamanism, the practitioner may wear a necklace of certain animal parts, bones, or even the antlers as a headdress all for either protection or to invoke the animal's traits as their own. This may not be for everyone and there are rules to follow. The parts must be acquired in an ethical way. Depending on where you live you may have access to found parts, such as snake skin which can be used in magic for transformation or crow feathers for creativity and guidance. These parts should always be cleaned before used and if you cannot do a traditional cleaning, then place the item in a bag and place it in the freezer for several days.

Animals are majestic and every animal has a purpose and a meaning. Figuring out what it means to you is the fun part. Remember, these creatures often come with a message and you must always approach with respect and at times caution. Never try to force an animal to be a part of your magical practices; they will come to you when the time is right.

Tools of the Witch

The use of tools in Witchcraft is very common, though it is possible to practice the Craft without the use of tools, they do help to increase power and focus. There are many items that can be used as magical tools however there are a few standard ones I will mention here.

Pentacle:

The pentacle is often the centerpiece of the altar. This is a five-pointed star enclosed in a circle. Often used as a place to charge items with energy, the pentacle can be made from many different materials. The base is often stone or wood and the star is either painted or engraved. Many practitioners will add other symbols to represent certain deities they may be working with. This piece is also used to summon certain Gods or Goddesses and is at times used to represent the elements; some see the pentacle as representing the element of earth.

Wand:

Yes, a Witch with a wand, quite a familiar site with the popularity of certain movies and television shows. Typically, a wand should be made from a sacred tree, like Elder, Oak, or Willow. The wand is used to direct energy, charge objects, draw down the moon, bestow blessings, and even control a summoned deity. Finding the right one for you is very personal. Some will make their wand from a chosen piece of wood, engrave personal power symbols on it, or add gems. There is also the belief that a wand should be from dead wood, fallen twigs etc. This ensures you are not harming a living tree and the wand was "given" to you in this manner. Most important, the wand should feel right for you, it should feel like an extension of yourself. This piece is believed to represent the element of air; some cultures use it to represent fire.

Athame:

This is the traditional dagger. This blade is used to direct the power we pass through it, to cast circles and to banish negative energy. This dagger is never used for cutting and has a black handle so as not to confuse it with a Boline, which is a more traditional cutting tool in Witchcraft. A Boline is used to carve wands, chop herbs, mark candles, and cut cords used in magic. The Athame is believed to represent the element of fire, while some use it to represent air.

Chalice:

This cup is another key part of an altar. Some believe it represents the womb of the Goddess; while other tools like the wand are thought to be masculine, this one is feminine. The base of the Chalice represents the material world, the stem represents the connection between ourselves and the Spirit, and the rim symbolizes the opening to receive spiritual energy. Blessed water or wine is often contained within and the cup itself is usually made of silver or pewter. This piece is believed to represent the element of water.

Cauldron:

Possibly the most well recognized tool of Witchcraft, the cauldron is also a symbol of the womb and fertility. This is used to make special herbal mixtures or brews to aid in magical endeavors, it can also be used for scrying by filling it with water and gazing into it as you would a crystal ball. Typically, these are made of cast iron and are considered a symbol of water as well as reincarnation and immortality.

Bell:

The bell is used for a few purposes. Often it is used to start a ritual, call the watchers of the four quarters, and even to ward off negative spirits and invite positivity. Bells are often hung in doorways and cupboards for this very purpose.

Finding and Cleansing Your Tools:

Tools can be bought from many New Age stores, though some prefer to let the tool find them or even make their own. When you do find something you wish to use for your altar, it is important that you cleanse it of all outside energy it may have come in contact with before it came to you. Some practitioners physically wash the tools in natural water from an ocean or lake, some bury them for a few days and let the earth absorb the old energy and some have other methods such as freezing the items. Whichever you choose, make sure it isn't going to ruin the item and be sure to consecrate the tools before they are used.

What Makes Magic "Black"?

The term Black Magic brings up many different questions and many misconceptions. Is Witchcraft Black Magic or Voodoo? What about Shamanism? The truth is that none of these immediately falls under the label of "black" or "dark" magic. In my experience, I've always felt magic is neither black nor white. It is all in the intent of the practitioner. Spell casting, rituals, and incantations all require energy that we, as the practitioner, must gather and release with our intent.

So, When Does Magic Turn Dark?

In no way am I saying Black Magic doesn't exist. It very much does, and what it requires is a great desire for personal gain regardless of who or what may be harmed in the process. I consider it more of dark intent than dark magic. Many see magic as a form of prayer. A series of actions that we hope will be witnessed and answered by unseen forces that are greater than we are. Who or what this higher power is varies on the form of magic being performed. Most practitioners understand there are rules, above all to never attempt to harm another living being. Some feel it is within their right to practice otherwise.

The Misuse of Magic

Any form of magic can be misused. The information that is available on how to manipulate common spells and turn them into something dark is astounding. Any tool, candle, herb, poppet, crystal, or stone can be used for selfish and harmful magic. To put things in perspective, let's think about more common items outside of the magical realm. We use cars for transportation, knives to prepare food, and tools like a hammer and screwdriver to repair things around the home. These are all things that most would not immediately think to use to cause harm to another; however, there are those who have used each of these things in harmful and malicious ways. Intent is what defines it all. I do believe there are people who both intentionally and unintentionally pursue Black Magic. Let's look at a few instances of the misuse of Black Magic. One such instance is when someone is angry or hurt and they wish to perform a spell to bring bad luck upon the one who wronged them. They aren't a bad person and probably aren't even thinking clearly about what they are doing. Usually, these people aren't very familiar with how the magical arts work and therefore, fortunately, fail at their attempt. Then there are people who pursue the magical talents of other "practitioners" who sell "curses," and they are conveniently able to "remove" a curse that may have been placed on you. These offers should be avoided for many reasons. Usually these are people looking to take advantage of the emotionally wounded and misguided. This brings me to those who know exactly what they are doing, advanced practitioners of the Dark Arts. This type of magic requires sacrifice, literally. Blood is viewed as the ultimate release of power. Rituals consist of everything from calling upon demons, manipulating the dead, and taking in the power of ancient deities for ultimate control. These practitioners are very much aware that there is great risk in what they are doing. Complete guides are available on working with demons and malicious entities. There is always an exchange for the abilities that are given, but the need for power and control is so great it is a small price to pay in the minds of some.

Only Use Spells and Rituals to Do Good

My personal belief is that spells and rituals should be used to send positivity and not for Dark Magic. Spells and rituals are tools to help carry out your intent of protection, good health, and clarity. The deities should be worked only if they are willing, and never to invoke into oneself. Entities, particularly inhuman, should never be called upon, in my opinion, especially with the intent to carry out your bidding. These entities are not to be trusted and will always have their own agenda. Nature is meant to be respected not manipulated and, most importantly, no living thing should be harmed in any way, shape, or form. Harm none. Remember, what you put forth will return. When love, compassion, and good will is sent out, you will see it come back to you in some way or another. When greed, destruction, and evil are the goal, the consequences can be disastrous. We can't stop people who pursue the Dark Arts, but we can educate ourselves to recognize what Black Magic is and help others understand. Proper knowledge is key.

Section 3

Urban Legends

Three Kings Ritual

We all want to know whom or what may be waiting on the "other side" but the question arises, how many other planes of existence are out there? Something else to take into consideration during our open willingness to tap into "other realms" is how close we are to the border of our plane and theirs. There has been a ritual growing in popularity that claims to assist the participant in reaching a place called the "shadow side" and allow them to gain knowledge and insight, though you run the risk of crossing over too far and possibly not being able to find your way back. This ritual is known as The Three Kings. I RECOMMEND THAT YOU DO NOT TRY THIS RITUAL.

Set Up

You are instructed to begin the set up for this ritual around 11 p.m. You are instructed to perform this ritual alone, but it is recommended that you have a loved one in the house who is aware of what you're doing, and they are going to help during the ending of the ritual. You must have a room set aside that is preferably windowless; if there are windows, cover them. Place three chairs in the room, one facing north (this is your throne), and the other two exactly to the left and right facing your throne. The chairs should be an arm's length away from each other. Take two large mirrors and place them at a 90-degree angle to the two chairs facing your throne. Once you are sitting, you should barely be able to see your own reflection in your peripheral vision; this means the setup is correct. Next, place a bucket of water and a cup in the center, just out of reach. Place a fan behind your throne, turn it on a medium or low setting, and leave it on. You are then instructed to turn off all lights and leave the room; make sure the door is left open. Also, make sure your cellphone is fully charged, and leave it next to your bed along with a candle and a lighter. Set an alarm for 3:30 a.m., and go to sleep while holding on to a cherished object; this will be known as your power object.

Beginning the Ritual

Once the alarm goes off, it is time to begin. Shut off the alarm, but do not turn the lights on. Light your candle, grab your cellphone and power object, and walk to your throne. You must be seated by 3:33 A.M., probably because the number three is associated with mind, body, and spirit. There are a few things to keep in mind. If your cellphone did not completely charge, do not proceed. If the door to the room you set up is closed, remember you left it open, do not proceed. If the fan is off, remember you left it on, do not proceed. If you are not seated by 3:33 A.M., do not proceed. These are all red flags, and you are then instructed to leave the house with your loved one until 6 A.M. However, if everything appears as it should be, you are instructed to continue.

Once you are seated, stare straight ahead; do not look at the candle's flame, and do not look into any of the mirrors. Sitting on your throne, the chairs to your left and your right are the Queen and the Fool. Keep in mind you are not alone, hence the name Three Kings. This is where experiences vary. The theory is you will have all your questions answered; however, should you believe anything from the fool? How do you know who to listen to or trust? There have been reports from people attempting this who have claimed everything from hearing low whispers to carrying on full conversations and even astral projecting to see themselves on the throne. Many have reported being in a deep trance-like state and having both beautiful and terrifying visions. Sitting in the dark with mirrors and candlelight is enough, on their own, to play with a person's mind, but is it all just a mind game?

Safety

Several things were placed as safety precautions for this ritual. Remember your body is in between the fan and your candle; if for some reason your body is physically moved or dragged from the throne, the fan will blow out the candle, ending the ritual. If for some reason you cross too far into the shadow side, your power object can help to guide you back. At 4:34 A.M., your loved one is instructed to call your name. If this does not work, they must call your cellphone. If you're still unresponsive, they must go into the room, but are not allowed to touch you. They must use the bucket of water and the cup to attempt to bring you back to our plane. The energy in water has long been used in magic, especially when the subconscious mind is at play.

Ending the Ritual

Once any of these things listed above has occurred, the ritual has officially ended. Cleanse the room used just to be on the safe side. There have been reports of lingering effects for several days or even weeks after participating in this ritual, such as vivid dreams or nightmares.

Curses, Jinxes, & Hexes

Curses, Jinxes, Hexes, is there a difference? Are they real? Throughout many cultures and religions there always seems to be some story of warning. Are these stories there just to ensure that we stick to a moral code?
Many practitioners of magic feel it is never a good idea to bring ill will intentionally, and even worse, harm to another human being, yet that is the sole purpose of a curse. However, I have come across Witches that consider themselves to be "pro-curse" and see no problem with the practice. Even more mind blowing are the profits some are making from not only the casting but also the removal of these curses. Yet the question remains are curses real or is it all in the power of fear we give them?

Curse, Jinx, Hex, What's the Difference?

The terms curse and jinx are used almost interchangeably. Each meaning you can cause someone to have bad luck, health, or worse just by speaking. If enough energy is put into the words, it is believed to give it enough power to carry the curse successfully. A hex is often described as something a little more ritualistic. You must gather certain items, hair, clothing, or personal objects to ensure the most power is put into your purpose of ill intent to an individual. Usually curses and hexes are viewed as a more ancient concept, though some modern practitioners still attempt to utilize them for revenge or personal gain.

Tutankhamun Curse

One of the most well-known "curses" involves king Tutt's tomb. Ancient Egypt was a very spiritual place, their kings were treated as Gods, and they were ensured to be very well protected and respected in the afterlife. Many tombs were believed to hold curses within them to protect the body and belongings from grave robbers or anyone else who may intrude. In 1922, an archeologist named Howard Carter returned to Egypt in search of King Tutt's tomb after several unsuccessful years. This time Carter brought with him a canary to aid in the search. This seemed to do the trick. After some digging, the steps were found that led to a sealed doorway with the name Tutankhamun. When Carter returned home that night, a servant met him holding yellow feathers in his hand. He reported a snake had killed the canary. He believed this was a sign and warned Carter not to continue his exploration of the tomb. The archeologist didn't believe in superstition and sent word to the wealthy Lord Carnarvon, who had been backing his research, to join him as he opened the tomb. On November 26th, the tomb was opened, revealing all of its treasures. However, shortly after, Lord Carnarvon died from an infected insect bite while in Cairo it was rumored during the time of his death that his dog back in England had suddenly passed. By 1929, the press had reported eleven associated with the opening of the tomb had died in unusual ways. However, later research had shown the press may have exaggerated to keep an audience engaged with the cursed tomb story. Even more interesting was the discovery years later that many illnesses that occurred may have been due to the mold that was in the tomb and not a mummy's curse.

Tomino's Hell

Tomino's Hell is a recent urban legend/curse. This is a Japanese poem written about a young boy and his descent into Hell. The poem is quite creepy with some disturbing imagery. However, it is advised to only read the poem in your mind and never out loud. Reading the piece aloud is believed to bring illness and possible death. People have reported feeling uneasy and nauseated after reading it, even silently. If the poem was not labeled as cursed would these feelings still occur in people?

James Dean's Cursed Car

In 1955, James Dean upgraded to a 550 Spyder and asked George Barris to customize the Porsche, and so he did. The creation was later nicknamed "Little Bastard" which was soon painted on the car. In September of 1955, Dean met with actor Alec Guinness to show him the car. Alec told him the car had a sinister appearance and if he didn't get rid of it, he'd be dead in a week. One-week later James Dean died in a car accident. George Barris bought the remains of the wrecked car. While transporting the wreckage the Spyder slipped off the trailer and broke a mechanic's leg. Soon Barris sold the engine and drivetrain to Troy McHenry and William Eschrid. While the two friends were racing, cars that contained the parts of "Little Bastard" both had serious accidents; McHenry was killed instantly while Eschrid was seriously injured. The two tires that were saved from the original accident were also sold but blew out simultaneously causing the new owner to crash. Barris still had most of the car less the parts he sold. Two thieves had tried to steal pieces such as the steering wheel and both sustained injuries. Barris wanted to hide the car away but was convinced to place it in a highway safety exhibit. The first garage the car was housed in burned to the ground, yet the "Little Bastard" had little fire damage. The car was later put on display at a high school and somehow fell, breaking a student's hip. Any truck attempting to either transport the "Little Bastard" has crashed or the car somehow breaks away from, or falls off the transporting trucks. Finally, when the car was supposed to be shipped back to Barris to finally rest, it somehow disappeared and never made it home. Some believe the car was "misplaced" on purpose.

Do You Believe In Mary Worth?

Mary Worth, Mary Worthington, Mary Whales and Hell Mary, these are all names given over time for one very popular legend. Trust me you know to whom I'm referring. If you haven't taken the dare yourself, you probably know someone who has. Usually performed during slumber parties or on a dark Halloween night, you all gather together in front of a mirror, wait; someone must turn off the lights. Now with a single candle, the brave chosen one stands in front of the mirror and slowly chants, Bloody Mary. The call supposedly brings forth the vengeful spirit.

Different Yet the Same

There are different variations to the ritual. The one I grew up with said you had to call her name three times in a darkened room, while standing in front of a mirror. Other interpretations include saying her name 13 times, spinning in circles, or adding to the chant antagonizing phrases like "Bloody Mary, I have your baby."

The outcome of what happens after the spirit is called also varies. There are tales of a spirit appearing and pulling the one who called her into the mirror. Other stories include a disfigured woman who scratches and claws at you, or the threat of the spirit haunting you for the rest of your life.

Who Was Mary?

Where did this legend come from and why would anyone want to bring the threat of an angry spirit to them? The origin has as many variations as the ritual itself. Some of the most popular theories are of a woman named Mary Worth who was disfigured in a horrible accident, and there is the thought that maybe she was a Witch burned at the stake. There was no Mary Worth or Mary Worthington during the Salem Witch trials, so the latter is not likely. Another tale tells of a woman who had her child taken from her and ended her life due to the grief, hence the belief that saying you have her child will bring her forth.

A couple of the more probable suspects in the mystery of Bloody Mary are based on people we know existed. Mary I Queen of England, who ruled during the Tudor period, was nicknamed Bloody Mary due to her many violent executions and burning people at the stake for heresy. This all took place in a short five-year period. Queen Mary was also unable to successfully bare children.

Elizabeth Bathory, though not named Mary is another woman that comes to mind in the creation of this legend. She was known as the Blood Countess or Blood Queen. In the early 1600's it was told that she would torture and kill young women, and then bathe in their blood. She believed this would preserve her youthful appearance.

Always in the Mirror

Regardless of the origin, this legend has survived time and distance. People of all ages all over the world are familiar with this ritual. The one thing these rituals have in common is the way people call upon her with the use of the mirror. Mirrors have been a common tool in divination and spirit communication for centuries. There are many superstitions regarding mirrors that I have mentioned in a previous article.

People enjoy being scared; enjoy the heart pounding excitement, and just want to be a part of something unique. Though, with any of the dares I always give the warning, be careful what you wish for you may not like the outcome.

Midnight Game

I came across The Midnight Game a few years ago while researching modern-day urban legends. I was very intrigued yet unsettled all at once. There seems to be almost a trend with these "rituals" that not only summon entities but also challenge them.

What Is the Midnight Game?

The goal of the game is to summon The Midnight Man, an entity that you must invite in and then avoid for a designated amount of time. Allowing the Midnight Man to catch you will result in hallucinations of your greatest fear. The origins of this ritual are difficult to trace. The instructions claim that this game was used by ancient Pagans to teach lessons in how to follow rules and respect the Elder Gods. Do I believe that? No. I think this may have just been the grand creation of someone who loves urban legends and just happened to create one that caught on. However, I still would never attempt this ritual. Going in with the intent of summoning an entity is never a good idea, and you never know who or what will answer.

How Is the Ritual Performed?

The rules require the participants to be in a location with a wooden door, and it is recommended the game be "played" with multiple people to ensure the best chance of escaping the entity. Participants must start a few minutes before midnight. Materials needed include a pencil, paper, candles, matches, salt, and a sewing needle or pin. Each player writes their full name, first, middle, and last, on a piece of paper with a pencil. Then the players each prick their finger, place a drop of blood on the paper with their name, and let it soak in. The rules specifically state never to use someone else's blood for your piece of paper; this will provoke the entity. Make sure all the lights are off in the house. Each player must now light their candles with a match, not a modern lighter. The participants place the paper with their name on it in front of a wooden door and place the candle on top of the paper. This is where timing is everything. Knock on the wooden door 22 times; each knock must match the ticking of the clock and the final knock should be at the exact moment midnight arrives. Now, open the door, blow out your candle, and close the door. This has summoned the Midnight Man.

What Happens Once the Midnight Man Is Summoned?

This is where the game begins. Light the candle again and keep moving throughout the house to avoid the entity until 3:33 A.M. If the Midnight Man is near, the candle will go out. If this happens, it must be relit within 10 seconds with a match. If the candle will not relight, place a circle of salt around where you're standing and stay within that circle for protection. For those who can relight their candle, they must keep moving; you are not allowed to stay in one spot. Flashlights are not allowed, you cannot turn on any lights until 3:33 A.M., and do not even think about falling asleep. Those who claim to have played this "game" have reported seeing a humanoid figure in the darkness, feeling a freezing cold chill, and hearing low whispers. Allowing the entity to catch up to you means you run the risk of being tortured with vivid hallucinations of your deepest, darkest fears.

How Do You Win the Game?

Once the clock hits 3:33 A.M. and you have avoided the entity, the game is over. You may turn on lights. You may want to do a cleansing of the house to ensure any negative energy is gone. Some claim to continue to feel watched for days or weeks after calling the Midnight Man.

One Man Hide and Seek

Recently, I have come across another urban legend that promises to summon a spirit, but this one is quite different. This "game" is more of a "ritual," and I was intrigued yet horrified at the details of it all. Spirit summoning is nothing to be taken lightly. The fact that I first read about this "game" on a site geared toward children was quite disturbing. Inviting the unknown can have disastrous consequences. There are many forces with powers beyond our comprehension at work that we, as human beings, do not realize until it is too late. Nevertheless, here are the details of this "game," though I do not recommend attempting it for any reason.

Hitori Kakurenbo

Hitori Kakurenbo, aka Hide and Seek by yourself, seemed to first appear on Japanese message boards around 2007 and gained popularity here in the States as One Man Hide & Seek a few years later. The purpose is to summon a spirit by offering a "body" for it to inhabit for a short period of time. Let's look at the details of this "game".

You're Not Alone

You're instructed to take a stuffed toy, one with arms and legs, remove the stuffing, and replace it with rice. The rules warn against using a doll that resembles a human for fear that the spirit may not want to leave this host. Replacing the stuffing with rice symbolizes an offering to the spirit. Give the toy a name; it cannot be your name or the name of anyone you know. Next, it is requested that you add something from your own body; usually this means fingernails or a piece of your hair. Some add to the ritualistic feel by placing a drop of their own blood into the toy. Next, sew the toy back together with red thread and bind the remainder of the thread around the body. The red thread is to symbolize blood vessels. Find a sharp object; you can use the needle, scissors, or a knife. Remember, the spirit could use against you once the "game" has begun. Fill a bathtub or sink with water, and make sure you have a glass of salt water nearby for yourself. Water has always been used as a portal and a way to increase spiritual energy. The salt water is for your own protection and will be used later to finish the ritual. Now you must select a hiding place; it is suggested you keep the salt water and your cell phone in your hiding place. Finally, turn the television onto a channel with static. The white noise is a way to hear if the spirit is nearby. Keeping doors and windows closed has been an optional choice. Some believe you should keep them open for easy escape in case things get dangerous; others suggest keep them locked to help contain the spirit. Begin the ritual at 3 A.M. This hour has always been associated with spirit activity. Make sure all the lights in the house are off; only the television should be on. Hold the toy and say three times, "I (your name) am the first it!" Place the toy in the water and go to your hiding spot. Count to 10, run back to the toy, pick it up and say, "I found you" and stab it with your sharp object. The rules suggest you sever as much of the red thread as possible. Now say, "You (toy's name) are now it!" Drop the doll back in the water, leave the sharp object, and run to your hiding place. Make sure the salt water is there with you. This is where experiences differ. You may wait for a long time and experience nothing. You may hear footsteps or the television may begin to switch channels. The channel flipping may begin to form sentences, such as, "Where are you?" or "I will find you!"

Ending the Game

When to end the "game" is up to you, though it is highly recommended not to exceed a few hours because the spirit may become too strong and more difficult to stop. Take a drink of the salt water and hold it in your mouth, carry the remainder of the water with you. The salt in the water will protect you as you search for the toy. Remember the toy and the sharp object may not be where you left it, so be cautious. Once you find the toy, spit the salt water onto it and say three times, "I win!" You may also want to pour the remainder of the salt water over it to ensure your protection. The toy should be burned and buried once the "game" is over. The truly frightening thing is this "game" is not the only one of its kind floating around. How many people are going to open doors that cannot be closed due to the misrepresentation of these rituals as harmless fun?

Seeking Answers from Other Realms

The desire to know what the future holds for our loved ones and us is only natural. The paths we take seeking such knowledge varies. Some take it lightly, reading their daily horoscope, or cracking open a fortune cookie. Then there are those that dig a little deeper, consulting with psychics, clairvoyants or tarot readers. Finally, there are those who go beyond, far beyond, into realms outside of our own.

Beyond the Ouija Board

Most common is with the use of the Ouija board, communicating with a ghost or entity in hopes of getting our questions answered. The theory is that the beings outside of our realm have the best knowledge of what can and will happen. These beings are part of a place we cannot see except for possibly in dreams; they can seamlessly and stealthily travel between our two worlds and even manipulate our reality. So why not go straight to the source? The danger involved is simply not worth the risk in my opinion. Some of the rituals require summoning something that is most likely not human. Dealing with non-human entities is something even a skilled practitioner may avoid doing at all costs. Proper opening and closing of the ritual is rarely done due to the fact these are presented as 'games' and the aftermath can be disastrous. New answer seeking rituals are popping up continuously; here are a few newer ones I've come across.

Little Devil

Said to have originated in Russia, this ritual has nothing to hide; the title alone says it all. The Little Devil is also known as Chertik. You are instructed to draw a perfect circle with a dot in the middle. Then, draw a devil with horns, tail and hooves, the dot should be at the chest; this will be the devils heart. The entire alphabet is written around the outside of the circle and numbers 0 – 9 are written inside the circle. The word "yes" is written at the devil's head and "no" at the feet. Light a candle and place it next to the drawing. You are then instructed to tie a piece of thread to a needle, place the needle in the candles flame and then dangle it above the paper so the tip of the needle is touching the devil's heart as you summon him. You must repeat the name 'Chertik, Chertik" when asking your questions and when you are done you must ask him to go away and burn the thread.

Satoru-Kun

This ritual comes from Japan, performing this is believed to summon a demon that presents itself as a young boy. Take your cell phone with you and seek out a public payphone. Use the payphone to dial your own cell phone number while reciting a certain chant asking Satoru-Kun to show himself and answer your question. Hang up the payphone and turn off your cell phone. If the ritual was successful, Satoru-Kun will call you within 24 hours. The first time he calls you, he will tell you where he is and hang up. Each time he calls you thereafter will reveal he is getting closer. On the final call, he will say, "I am behind you now"; you must ask your question without hesitation. The rules state you mustn't summon Satoru-Kun if you do not have a question, you mustn't turn around to look at him, and you mustn't try to touch him. Breaking these rules would result in your demise.

Answer Man

This is a recent one that has just been circulating over the last decade again originating from Japan. A group of ten people is instructed to sit in a circle. Each person must have their cell phone and know the phone number of the person sitting to their left. On the count of three, everyone must call this person, as they hold the phone to their ear and listen. Since everyone is doing this, all phones should be in use and therefore no one should hear an answer. However, if one person does hear the line pick up, they will hear the voice of the Answer Man. Now, they can ask whatever question they like. The Answer Man may ask a question in return, if the question is not answered correctly, the participant runs the risk of losing a part of their body. The legend states the Answer Man was born deformed and is looking for body parts to make himself whole again.

Summoned by the Internet

Today we do everything online; pay bills, make appointments, and get answers and opinions on almost anything. So, it is no surprise that there are now websites and YouTube videos that allege they can haunt or even curse you just by witnessing them, but, is it possible for a spirit or dark energy to have an effect via the web? Here are a few examples.

Repleh Snatas

This website has been around for several years. The story goes, Repleh Snatas was a young girl who was abused and tragically died. If you go to the website, you can summon her and she will invite you to come back at midnight. When you return she will ask you if you want to play. Clicking through a series of puzzles, creepy pictures and sound effects will eventually lead you to a screen where you can enter a name. Choose carefully, the name you enter must be someone you wish to harm. Repleh will carry out your wish but in return she will haunt your dreams for the rest of your life. Repleh Snatas is Satan's Helper backwards.

WPKEPKW

This bizarre title is known as "the Cursed YouTube video". The original upload date is not known because it allegedly keeps disappearing and the original video is said to be difficult to find. This is a short video, less than 30 seconds, and is simply a blurred image of what appears to be a human face. The features are indistinguishable and there is a dull noise in the background. There are reports the video causes fear and paranoia but that could be just a natural reaction the human brain has to an unrecognizable image.

The interesting and creepy part comes from another YouTuber who recorded the "curse" of this video. They recorded themselves just browsing another webpage when suddenly that blurred face would pop up on their screen out of nowhere. Other reports say hat along with this face a date will pop up, this is the date of your death. Another user who suggested the original proof of the intruding face was created with simple editing software reportedly debunked this. Either way the video is very unsettling. The image does stay with you once seen.

Suicide Mouse.avi

This video was uploaded in 2012 but is believed to feature animation from the 1930s. You begin by watching what appears to be an old Mickey Mouse cartoon. The mouse is walking along with buildings passing in the background on a continual loop. Mickey seems sad and the music in the background is a low depressing tune. Soon the scene begins to change slightly, buildings begin to warp and things become distorted. The music turns to a steady white noise and then the sound of a woman screaming a terrifying tortuous scream. The scene cuts out and a Russian text appears on the screen that reads "The sights of Hell bring its viewer back in". This video is believed to induce depression and suicidal thoughts. A rumor circulates around the clip stating someone did kill themselves after viewing; the last thing the victim said was "Real suffering is not known".

Mereana Mordegard Glesgorv

This video arrived in 2008 and has been taken down and re-uploaded many times. If you decide to watch this clip, you will first see everything in a red tint and a man staring at the camera. Soon the man's facial expression changes into a sinister smile and a low evil laugh can be heard in the background followed by bells. His eyes begin to dance and roll around, and everything is still drenched in red, while he keeps smiling. The reason this strange video gained a reputation is quite disturbing. Allegedly, upon its original upload over 100 people attempted to gouge their own eyes out after viewing. YouTube removed the video after these reports but it continues to be available and viewed. Many report not being able to complete the video due to the intense feeling of fear and general unease.

I have viewed these videos but not in their entirety. There are many theories and ways to debunk these clips but even if their sole purpose is to make you feel scared, paranoid or just completely uncomfortable, they succeeded. Can a video or website curse you? The power of the human mind is incredible especially combined with the power of suggestion.

The Evolution of the Urban Legend

Everyone has heard one form or another of the Urban Legend. They are told around campfires, or at slumber parties. Scary stories of ghosts, crazed lunatics, and bizarre occurrences. Why are we so drawn to them? The origin of the story is always vague and some details may change but the root of the story is always the same, to scare and shock. Usually these stories leave us questioning if this did, or could, this really happen.

Out with the Old

What is interesting is how these stories have evolved due to the advancements in modern technology. We remember the legends from the older generations. Like the babysitter who keeps getting strange phone calls, an eerie voice telling her to check on the children. She soon realizes the calls are coming from within the house. Or, the ghostly stories such as someone picking up a lone hitchhiker, having a full conversation then suddenly the passenger becomes quiet, as the driver turns to look the hitchhiker is gone.

Yet now, with cell phones and the internet, the legends we knew as kids are mere child's play in comparison. Modern technology gives us the opportunity to reach out to almost anyone, yet we never seem to question who or what can reach back. Spirits have been known to communicate through baby monitors, televisions and cameras, so why not computers?

Creepypastas

These new internet urban legends are called Creepypastas and they are everywhere. The word is a play on the term "copypasta" which is slang for the action of copying & pasting a story and passing it around the internet. These have become so common that a new generation of monsters have been created from these stories. Now names like Slenderman, Jeff the Killer and Smile Dog are household names. Some of them even bring a new twist to the old chain letter. Remember those letters we used to get before everything was through email and text, the ones that said if you don't pass this along to 5 or 10 people you'll have bad luck? Well now, these are chilling stories usually drawing you in with pity. You'll read about a young girl who was bullied, it was taken too far and her peers accidentally killed her. As you proceed, you will be warned that since you have read her story, you must forward it to let others know, or her ghost will appear to you and kill you as revenge.

With the advancements in video, there are several Creepypastas of haunted video games or children's cartoons. These stories always involve someone getting a game or old copy of a classic cartoon. They take it home and settle in for some recreation. The fun turns to terror as the familiar scenes change and the beloved characters become angry or agitated and begin doing things that are not part of the script, dark, disturbing things. Soon the person who witnessed the horror will be haunted, not only by the images but sometimes by a ghost or demon, apparently summoned by the strange scenes.

Funny Mouth

One of the creepiest ones I have read recently is the story of Funny Mouth. This is a rather long tale that describes a young man who is up late chatting online with friends. An unknown user with the name Funny Mouth pops up and starts saying things that seem strange and senseless. The young man briefly engages and only gets the emoticon for "staring" in return. He ignores Funny Mouth and goes to bed. He soon has a nightmare of lying in the grass and feeling a worm crawl on his neck. He wakes up to feel dampness on his neck but passes it off as drool. Soon he receives emails from Funny Mouth saying, "I see your handsome face." and "You'll like it." so he blocks him. Then when he tries to log in to his website, he sees Funny mouth has hacked it and only an image of a blurry face with a distorted jaw appears. The young man emails Funny Mouth back, threatening him and demanding he turn the site back to normal. That night he has a similar nightmare with the worm on his neck. The worm crawls up towards his mouth and he realizes it is not a worm but fingers, reaching in and pulling down. He cannot wake himself up. Finally, he awakens, runs to the bathroom to look in the mirror. The bright light blurring the vision of his face in the mirror but his jaw, dislocated, he starts laughing uncontrollably as he thinks "What a handsome face, what a funny mouth." The creator of the story has even included a fun interactive twist. If you go to the website mentioned in the original story, a page stating it is under construction will greet you. Exiting out and going back in will reveal the same horrific image the young man in the story saw on his computer.

Endless Possibilities

These new urban legends have changed the way we view our daily life. That random friend request from someone you do not know, the lone book that catches your eye because it seems out of place from the rest, or that time your cell phone camera had a "glitch" and revealed a strange image, these are all how Creepypastas begin.

Section 4

Paranormal

Annabelle

One of my all-time favorite "ghost" stories is about a Raggedy Ann doll named Annabelle. The story begins in 1970; a mother purchased the child size doll at a hobby store as a present for her daughter Donna who was a nursing school student at the time. She lived in a small apartment with her roommate Angie. Donna loved the doll and placed it on her bed but this didn't seem to be where Annabelle wanted to stay.

Small Changes

Over a short period of time, the girls noticed Annabelle would be moved slightly. Very small changes in positions at first but still noticeable, especially since neither one of them had touched her. Then the movements became more bizarre. Donna and Angie would come home to find Annabelle in a completely different room than where they left her. No one else had been in the house but there the doll sat on the couch with her legs crossed or sometimes even standing upright, leaning on a chair. If they left Annabelle on the couch and stepped out, they would return to find her back on Donna's bed with the door closed.

Spirit Notes and The Search For Answers

Several weeks into the doll's stay, pieces of parchment paper were found around the apartment. Neither Donna nor Angie had any parchment paper in the house and had no idea where it was coming from. To add to the mystery there was what seemed to be a child's writing scribbled on the paper reading, "help us" or "help Lou." Lou was a close friend to the girls and soon the message would be all too clear.

After another one of Annabelle's "moving" episodes, Donna noticed what appeared to be blood on the dolls hands and chest, now scared and not knowing where to turn they contacted a Medium and a séance was held. During the séance, it was told that a spirit of a young girl named Annabelle Higgins was the one living in the doll. She said that she had died in a field where the apartment now stands and felt safe with Donna and Angie. Annabelle wanted to stay and Donna gave her permission to do just that, a choice they would later come to regret.

Nightmare or Reality?

Now back to Lou. One night, while taking a nap in the apartment, he began to have what seemed like a nightmare though he was sure he was awake, yet he couldn't move. Looking around the room, he had a strange, eerie feeling. Lou looked down to see Annabelle gliding up his leg. When she got to his chest, she stopped. Soon Lou felt as if he couldn't breathe, as if he was being strangled. Could the doll possibly be choking him? Soon he blacked out, waking up that morning; he insisted this was no nightmare. Annabelle continued to attack Lou, on one occasion leaving claw marks on his chest.

The Warrens

Once the doll seemed to have malicious intent, Donna contacted an Episcopal priest, the priest contacted a higher authority in the church, and that higher authority contacted paranormal investigators Ed and Lorraine Warren. After listening to everyone's experiences the Warrens concluded that the doll was not haunted by the ghost of a little girl but manipulated by an inhuman and demonic entity. The demon tricked Donna and Angie into believing there was the spirit of a scared little girl in the doll so they would give it permission to stay in the home. The demon was using the doll to gain recognition and eventually try to find a human host. The Warrens made the decision to take the doll with them.

With Annabelle in the backseat and the entity still attached and very angry, it began to attack. The car would swerve with every turn, it would stall and the brakes would fail. The Warrens were able to avoid a collision; after Ed stopped the car long enough to throw Holy Water on the doll, the car was back to normal. They arrived home and placed Annabelle in a chair near Ed's desk. The doll would levitate and within a few weeks began showing up in different rooms.

She is Listening

A special case was built for Annabelle in the Warren's Occult Museum in Monroe Connecticut. While in her case, she doesn't seem to move any longer but she is still believed to be something one must respect. Several years ago, while touring the museum a young man began to taunt Annabelle. He was tapping on the glass and daring her to do something. Ed asked the man to leave. While riding his motorcycle home, the young man collided into a tree and died. His girlfriend survived the accident and said the last thing she remembers was how they were laughing and joking about the doll.

Clinton Road

Have you ever been driving late at night down a dark road and it seems there is no civilization for miles? You think to yourself how this would be a great scenario for a horror movie, yet all the while hoping you're not part of the horror. There is a road known as one of the scariest roads in America. Clinton road in West Milford New Jersey has quite a reputation from as early as 1905.

Ghost Boy

Clinton road is a simple two-lane road, surrounded by woodland with many ghost stories. One of the most famous stories is near the bridge. There is the tale of a young boy with some conflicting details; some tell of the boy drowning, others say that he was hit by a car going down the road. If you drop a coin into the water, it is believed the coin will be tossed back up to you. Another legend states if you leave the coin in the center of the yellow line in the road the same will happen. A more terrifying twist on the tale is if you lean to look over the bridge, the boy may push you, attempting to get you off the road and away from oncoming cars.

Horrific History

There have been numerous accounts of strange activity, murders, and robbery. People have claimed to see bonfires in the woods surrounding the road, stories of Satanists performing rituals and even KKK gatherings. Back in 1983, a body was discovered in the woods by a bicyclist. This was one of many victims of Richard Kuklinski also known as the "Iceman". Kuklinski was given the nickname because he froze the bodies of his victims to make it seem as if they died at a later time than they actually did. When an autopsy was performed on the victim found near Clinton Road, they discovered ice crystals near the blood vessels in his heart.

If ghost children, murderers, and cults aren't enough, there have been stories of strange creatures being spotted on this road. In 1976, a Jungle Habitat attraction closed and it was believed many of the animals escaped and crossbred. Bizarre monkey-like creatures, large rabbits and even "hell hounds" are reported to dart across the road.

Ghost Car

What would stories of a scary road be without reports of a ghost car? One tale tells of a phantom Camaro with a ghostly female driver who died when she crashed the car in 1988. There is a theory that any mention of these stories at night will trigger a manifestation, possibly it just triggers the imagination, either way many take the dare to drive this road at night. For several miles, there is nothing but darkness and the sight of your own headlights. Many do this in hopes of triggering another famous legend of Clinton Road.

Imagine coming up to the large curve known as "Dead Man's Curve". There is now railing put up along the side because many have driven off this curve and died. Yet this does not seem to help, why? Well, did I mention the Ghost Truck?

Tailgating

Here you are taking this long dark drive when suddenly headlights appear in your rear-view mirror. There seems to be a driver behind you, they seem to be in a hurry. The truck tailgates, backs off then rushes the back of your car again. They are driving erratically, swerving, and yet they never go around you. This truck seems almost to want to make you veer off this road. You continue to speed up but the driver behind you will not back off and is getting aggressive, you can even hear their engine revving. Finally, you reach the light to the main highway, you feel you have reached civilization again, suddenly you notice the headlights that were relentlessly following you have disappeared, vanished like there was never another car behind you at all. There more than likely wasn't another car; you have just encountered the infamous Ghost Truck. Seen as either a white or a red truck, this has been one of the most common experiences of this spooky road.

Lonesome Road

Maybe it is the way our mind takes in the sight of a long, dark, seemingly endless road. As humans, we need to see light, a goal to pursue. When that doesn't seem within reach, we tend to get a feeling of dread and discomfort. Knowing all the legends can fuel the imagination. Tell me, would you drive down Clinton Road?

Doppelganger

Have you ever heard the theory that we all have a twin? The thought that there may be someone out there who looks and acts exactly as we do only it is not us at all. To some this is a mere urban legend, the myth of the Doppelganger.

However, is this really a myth? There may be some truth to this bizarre phenomenon. A look back reveals there have been some recorded cases in history of people seeing and even interacting with these "other halves".

What Is a Doppelganger?

The word is German for "double goer" or "double walker". Similar is the Vardoger from Scandinavian folklore, which describes a spirit predecessor. The doppelganger is believed to be much more sinister. Seeing your exact double is said to be a bad omen, a sure sign of misfortune or even death.

An example of such an encounter involved Abraham Lincoln. Shortly after his election in 1860, Mr. Lincoln was relaxing in his chamber one evening. He glanced toward a mirror and saw his reflection but with two separate faces. One face matched his perfectly while the other looked very pale and sickly. When the President walked to the mirror to examine further, the image disappeared only to reappear once he returned to his lounge. Bothered by the strange occurrence, he mentioned it to his wife later that evening. She expressed her fears that it could mean he would not live to see a second term.

The School Teacher

A very popular story of bi-location tells the story of a schoolteacher named Emilie Sagee in 19th century France. While writing on the chalkboard, Emilie's double appeared beside her, witnessed by her entire classroom of 13 students. The image was exact except it wasn't holding a piece of chalk. This was not the only time Emilie's doppelganger was seen. One day there were 42 students in the school's hall for a sewing class, they could see Ms. Sagee outside in the garden gathering flowers. When the sewing teacher stepped out of the room, the image of Emilie Sagee slowly began to appear in the teacher's chair, it sat motionless. The students could clearly see Ms. Sagee was still outside in the garden, though she began to look very tired and weak. A couple of brave students attempted to approach the apparition but said it felt as if there was a strange force around it, preventing them from getting too close. Emilie said she never saw the apparition herself but admitted to feeling very drained of energy whenever it made these appearances.

The Poets

John Donne, a poet during the 16th century, described seeing his wife's doppelganger while he was in Paris. The image was holding a baby and appeared to be very sad. His wife was pregnant at the time. John soon discovered, at the very moment he saw the image; his wife gave birth to a stillborn child.

Another English poet, Percy Shelly met his exact image while in Italy. The ghostly double silently pointed out towards the Mediterranean Sea. He later described the strange experience to friends and family. Soon after in 1822, Percy died in a sailing accident at that exact location.

The Lore

There are different variations of what a doppelganger is and why it appears. There is an old legend that describes evil imps or faeries that would steal healthy babies and replace them with sickly ones. Some believe that since everyone has a good and bad side, these entities are obviously the "bad" versions of us. Another thought is the doppelganger is stuck in another time and it allows us a brief glimpse into the future.

These stories may be just that, stories. Our own reflections have always inspired deep discussions of the symbolism of our own subconscious and our "true selves". People are often afraid to search within themselves and reveal things that may be seen as unfavorable. Who better to pass these qualities onto but a ghost? However, the theory of a "double walker" has inspired many stories and poems from all over the world and will probably continue to inspire and tempt the future generations.

Famously Haunted Disneyland, Anaheim, CA.

Disneyland has always been known as the happiest place on earth, yet as with most historic places, there is a dark side. There are many stories of haunting in the Magic Kingdom. A friend of mine was a former cast member of Disneyland and here are some of the accounts from him and a few other employees.

Walt, Are You Here?

When we first enter the park, we are greeted by a regal statue of Walt Disney himself, welcoming us to his land, his creation, and the place where, some say, he still resides. There is a train, engine #2, said to have been Walt's favorite. Mr. Disney loved trains and cast members who have worked on this engine report that before going through the tunnel that leads to the Toon Town Station, the bell will ring by itself. Some feel and possibly hope it is Walt himself letting them know he is still a part of the park. Another story from the train tracks is of an old engineer seen wearing train conductor clothing walking the tracks from the overpass between the park entrance and Main Street, only to disappear. There have been no reports of any conductors meeting their demise along these tracks, but since the park's opening in 1955, it is possible that one of the first conductors may have since passed on and may just be returning to the place they knew best.

Haunted Lands

Ironically, Tomorrowland has the most reported deaths than any other section. One tragic story is of Thomas

Cleveland, a 19-year-old who tried to sneak in to a Grad night celebration back in 1966. He climbed the fence and ended up on the tracks of the Monorail. A guard saw the boy and a quickly approaching Monorail. He yelled to the boy who attempted to jump to a canopy below the track but didn't make it in time. Now there are reports of a young boy seen walking the tracks until the Monorail approaches, then disappears.

Another interesting tale takes place in Fantasyland. There is a story of a woman named Dolly Young. Dolly is seen near the break room of the Matterhorn. She lost her life on this ride when she was thrown from her seat after unfastening her seatbelt.

One of the most popular, and my personal favorite, sections of Disneyland is New Orleans Square. This is where we find the Pirates of the Caribbean and Haunted Mansion ride. There is an unconfirmed story of the ghost of a young boy who is seen on the security cameras riding the boat in Pirates of the Caribbean. There has been one confirmed death on this ride but no connection to the story of the young boy.

Real Haunted Mansion

Still, one of the better-known ghost stories is of the real haunting in the Haunted Mansion. The story tells of a mother who brought her young son's ashes to the ride and asked to spread them there since it was his favorite. When her request was denied, she found a way to do it anyway and the ashes blended well with the dusty appearance of the ride. There have been reports of a little boy seen crying near the exit ramp. There are different versions of this story; others state the young boy helps in the loading queue by closing the doom buggies. There are a few authentic pieces of haunted history in the mansion. During the scene with the phantom piano player and the dead bride, a chest sits in this scene as well. The chest is from a home in Northern California and is believed to be haunted. When Walt Disney heard of it, he knew it would be perfect for the attraction. Those who have visited the mansion may have also noticed the hearse that sits just outside, it was rumored to be the actual hearse of Brigham Young but these are just rumors as this hearse was constructed, from scratch, at the Walt Disney Studios in Burbank, California.

Disneyland has always been a place for magic and wonder, where anything seems possible. These stories of ghosts and haunting are difficult to find but they lead to other possibilities. If these stories were publicized more, would it deter guests from visiting, or would it bring in even more people with a completely new reason to visit the Magic Kingdom?

Famously Haunted Hollywood

As a native of Southern California, it was only natural for me to combine my fascination with the paranormal and my love of old Hollywood. There are so many ghost stories that tinsel town has to offer. Perhaps it is because Hollywood has always been a place filled with passion and desire; such strong emotions are bound to leave a lingering impression. First, I would like to start with an interesting story that strangely combines two Hollywood tragedies that took place 37 years apart from each other.

Bombshell Tragedies

The blond bombshell actress Jean Harlow became famous for her lead role in the Howard Hughes film Hell's Angels. She married an assistant named Paul Bern in 1932. Their home was in the middle of 5 acres in Beverly Hills' Benedict Canyon. Sadly just a few months after the wedding, Bern committed suicide in his new wife's bedroom. Jean passed away 5 years later of kidney failure. Now, let us fast forward to 1966. The Harlow home had new occupants, Jay Sebring and his houseguest, a beautiful actress by the name of Sharon Tate. One-night Sharon could not sleep; she was alone for the evening and decided to stay in Jay's room. Suddenly, a figure of a thin man came into the bedroom, ignored her, and seemed to be looking for something. Sharon knew the history of the home and thought this presence could be Bern himself. She hurried out of the room and on the way downstairs, saw another apparition, a person tied to the post of the steps and brutally murdered. The vision soon vanished. Many believe Bern was attempting to warn Tate of what was to occur three years later when she would be a victim to the Manson family murders.

Falling Star

Even the Hollywood sign itself has a haunted past. There have been numerous reports called in to the local police department from concerned citizens who say they see a woman climbing the letter H of the Hollywood sign. When police arrive, there is never anyone there. Yet, in 1932, an actress by the name of Peg Entwistle was frustrated at never receiving her big break. She took a walk up the hillside and climbed the letter H by way of a ladder left behind by a workman. She then leapt to her death. This is a perfect example of a residual haunting, reliving those last few moments repeatedly to the horror of unsuspecting witnesses.

Haunted Hotel

Another occurrence that can stir up paranormal activity is any remodeling or heavy construction to a building that held strong energy to begin with. A perfect example of this is the Hollywood Roosevelt Hotel. This hotel, constructed in 1927, was designed to appeal to the movie industry at the time. The hotel's restoration process took place in 1984 and in 1985, the first stories of ghosts began to unfold. A mirror that once hung in room 1200, a room that was frequented by Marilyn Monroe, is said to be haunted by Marilyn herself. People have said they see a reflection of a blond woman in the mirror. Some feel it holds an imprint of the actress's tragic and restless spirit. Montgomery Clift also stayed in this hotel. He spent three months in room 928 while making the film From Here to Eternity in 1952. Clift would often play the bugle in between rehearsing his lines. The sound of a bugle can still be heard from this room and visitors may often feel a cold chill brush passed them in the corridor since Clift was known to pace the floor constantly.

God Isn't Here

There are so many stories of restless spirits and bizarre occurrences, for example, Joan Crawford's home was believed to have many spirits. There were reports of children laughing and shadows seen. Several exorcisms were performed on the home to no avail. Many thought Joan herself was possessed by something from within the house to explain her erratic behavior. Her last words were "Don't you dare ask God to help me." After Joan's passing, another family moved into the home and they too experienced strange things like fires erupting without a cause. They too called for an exorcism without success.

Hollywood will always be a place of great hope and great mystery. Yet some of the best stories do not require a script, just an open mind and an interest in the roles that are played after death.

Famously Haunted Queen Mary, Long Beach, California

The Queen Mary, also known as the Grey Ghost, is in the Long Beach Harbor. I have been lucky enough to visit this ship on several occasions and have had wonderful experiences each time. There is such a rich history behind the ship yet it has become more famous in its current state as a "Haunted Hotel". Why is the Queen Mary Haunted? Let us start with her early days as a luxury liner.

In the Beginning

The Queen Mary's construction began in 1930, yet her first voyage was not until 1936 due to delays caused by the Great Depression. The ship hosted some of the top movie stars and political figures of the day but the luxury liner only lasted for 3 short years. During the start of World War 2, the Queen Mary became a troop transport; it was then labeled the Grey Ghost.

One of the earliest tragedies with the Grey Ghost took place during the war. While attempting to avoid enemy ships she collided with a smaller companion ship nearly severing it in half, nearly 300 people were left for dead. Screams and pounding are said to still be heard on the ships fore hull.

In 1947, the ship was re-launched as a luxury liner, making weekly trips between England and New York. In 1967, she was sold to the city of Long Beach, California to be used as a museum and hotel. This is where the beautiful 1,000-foot long ship has rested since. Tourists from all over the world have come to view the splendor and maybe give in to the curiosity of the 150 plus spirits said to haunt the ship.

Ghostly Guests

The boiler and engine rooms of the ship have some of the most widely experienced activity. There is a story of a young man named John Pedder who was crushed by door 13 during a routine drill. There have been reports of people seeing a young man in blue overalls near this area as well as disturbances, such as cameras shutting off, batteries draining and so on. These disturbances are common in the paranormal field since it is believed spirits need to pull energy from around them to manifest

The swimming pool has also been known as a hot spot for activity. There have been reports of wet footprints when the pool has been empty and out of use for quite some time, as well as childish laughter. The spirit of a little girl named Jackie is said to frequent the pool area calling for her mommy. She is believed to have drowned back in the ship's luxury liner days. This is the area where I also had an interesting experience. During a tour, I was at the back of the line and doing a bit of lagging to take in the atmosphere. I felt a low and gentle tug on my purse, like a child reaching and wanting attention, I turned expecting to see the source but there was no one there.

There is also activity in other parts of the ship. A man in a 1930s style suit is seen near the first-class staterooms, as well as faucets turning off and on by themselves and phones ringing with no one on the other end. A young woman is also seen dancing by herself in the Queen's Salon, formally known as the first-class lounge.

More Personal Experiences

During one of my stays on the ship, I witnessed the sounds of children running and laughing down the hallway, yet there was never anyone in sight. While walking on the deck late at night, I would stop and hear what sounded like footsteps walking behind me yet I was alone. I plan to make another trip very soon now that there are so many new and exciting tools for paranormal investigation. I hope to be able to document some of my experiences.

Ghost hunting Basics for Beginners

Ghost hunting has gained increased popularity over the years due to recent movies and television series'. Paranormal investigation is no longer something strange or unusual; in fact, it is becoming not only a hobby but also, at times, a career choice. There are several things to consider when entering the world of ghost hunting. Many enter this field because they have unanswered questions regarding the afterlife, or just want to experience something that proves there is so much more out there than we are led to believe. Whatever the reasons, there must be an understanding of the rules and guidelines to paranormal investigations.

Location

First, pick your location. Do the proper research on what type of entity you are searching for and what the experiences have been in the past. This will help you prepare for the actual investigation. Always get permission to be on the property, never trespass under any circumstances. If you are unfamiliar with the area, you may want to visit the location during the day to avoid any potential hazards in the dark. Try to avoid visiting locations alone, not only is it better to have multiple sets of eyes to review potential evidence but it is just safer. Always make sure someone who isn't going to be with you knows where you are heading and there is a way to contact them if needed.

Preparation

Second, get prepared. Be sure to dress comfortably and wear good walking shoes. Try not to wear any cologne or perfume so as not to affect other people in your team. Some experiences center around scent, such as an entity carrying the smell of roses, smoke, sulfur and so on. Keep supplies to a minimum if it's only a small group, larger groups can carry more tools but make sure to have a comfortable and convenient way to carry them. There are many ghost-hunting gadgets out there but some of these things can get expensive. Start out with the basics. A flashlight, a pencil and notepad to make notes or reference back to previous research, a camera (either film or digital), a voice recorder, extra batteries, baby powder (works great to capture ghostly footsteps), water, and of course a first aid kit. Some investigators will also bring something for spiritual protection. Use whatever makes you feel comfortable based on your belief system. If you are feeling sick, depressed or generally under the weather, DO NOT proceed with the investigation. Ghosts need energy to manifest and may often try to use yours. Dizziness or disorientation is sometimes reported during ghost hunts, if you are already drained from the beginning this can be very dangerous to continue.

Investigation

Third, investigate. Once you have arrived at your location be sure to have a plan with your group and, if possible, try not to separate. Make sure you have referenced what you are looking for but try not to narrow your focus. Many times, experiences occur that are different from previous reports. Remember what type of entity are you searching for, is it a residual or intelligent haunting, is it known to be shy, friendly, or ill tempered, are there certain things you can say or do safely to increase the chances of it appearing, is there a language the entity understands best, and is it a human or non-human entity. Some people like to say or do something for protection before starting an investigation, but this is up to you. I have seen some investigators make a clear statement that any entities are not allowed to attach themselves or follow them once they leave.

Audio and Visual

Make sure to take numerous pictures, do not just click once if you hear a strange sound, point and shoot randomly and often, you will have a lot to review later but it will increase your chances of seeing something paranormal. When using the voice recorder, be sure to speak clearly, any whispering done by you and your team may sound like potential evidence later. Find a "hot spot" or a location known for heavy activity and use your voice recorder to ask questions, allow enough time for an answer. You may not hear anything at the time you're investigating, but upon review, you may discover an EVP or Electronic Voice Phenomena. Once you feel you have thoroughly investigated your location, make sure you clean up anything left over and head home. Since many investigations are done at night, you may want to wait until the next day to review everything. Never look for evidence with tired eyes.

The Review

Fourth, review. This can be the most tedious and yet most exciting part of the process. Examine your pictures and listen to your recordings. If anything unusual is heard or seen, have a second and even a third person review it as well. Take into consideration anything that may have contaminated the film or audio; was the investigation outdoors, and were there animals, traffic lights, or other people that could have made the picture or sound seem ghostly? If the investigation was indoors, was it an old building, was there faulty plumbing or electrical outlets. If none of these is a possibility, you may even have to return to the same location to try to recreate what was seen or heard.

Most of all have fun, try not to go into an investigation fearful, sometimes our own imaginations can run away with us and everything seems spooky like some old haunted house film with creaking doors and screeching owls.

Just relax and enjoy the experience. Do not be disappointed if your first few investigations turn up with no ghostly results. Some experienced investigators have several occasions with no results. Each ghost hunt is a chance to try new techniques, test new equipment, and see new places; it's all about opening your mind to the unknown.

Ghost Photography for Beginners

Just typing the words "ghost on film" into any search engine will bring up thousands of photos containing "ghosts" or "spirits". Many can prove quite disappointing when authenticity is a factor. With modern technology, almost anyone who has spent time with Photoshop can create a convincing "ghost" photo. Before the digital age when film was developed, or let's not forget the Polaroid, many believed a ghost was captured whenever a blur, streak, or double exposure appeared. So how can we tell what is real and what is fake?

Real or Fake?

Research is important. Examine as many "ghost" photos as possible, the good and the bad. Some will be obvious as fakes. A few famous ones that have recently circulated are one of a young man standing outdoors with a "ghost girl" standing eerily behind him. The girl is nothing more than a digitally placed image of the famous staple from most Japanese horror films. You know the type, long dark hair, usually covering the face, gaunt skeleton like features, and a look of terror in her eyes. The image appears in many "ghost photos" which is one of the first indications that it is not real, and second the image is very clear. Usually in the rare occasion a spirit does appear it is usually transparent and very rarely a full body with distinct features. When this does happen, it usually isn't long enough for the spirit to pose for the camera.

From The Movies

Another popular photo circulated several years ago, as part of a chain letter. The photo shows a girl in a hospital bed with a frightening looking woman lying directly underneath. Once again, the woman has a terrified look on her face with very gaunt features. The letter circulated via email or some social networking sites and stated that once it was viewed you had to send the photo to at least five other people or the woman under the bed would come to you that night. While a good ghost story, the photo was nothing more than a movie poster from a Thai horror film.

Orbs?

Many "ghost" photos contain orbs. These are circular objects believed to appear when a spirit is attempting to manifest itself. These round transparent objects are thought to be energy. Unfortunately, a majority of these "orb" photos are taken outside or in very old locations and dust particles can create the exact same image on film. Unless the orbs are forming together to create a shape or moving independently in a specific pattern, it is more than likely just dust.

Pareidolia

Other photos contain captions that tell you what to look for. Like a face over someone's shoulder or demonic hands reaching out from a wall. Usually these are simply shadow play or a double exposure making someone appear transparent. This uses the mind's ability to see whatever is suggested. If you were to observe the photo without the suggestion of a ghostly shadow, you more than likely wouldn't see one, but to observe the photo with the shadow circled and highly magnified with the caption stating there is a ghostly face, the mind will look for that exact thing. This is simply human nature, to attempt to make sense of the image, similar to finding shapes in clouds.

Practice

When I visit a reportedly haunted location, I take many pictures. Often, I'll snap the same picture several times. There is always a lot to go through upon review but this helps to sharpen skills in looking for subtle changes. When something odd is seen on a picture, I ask myself several questions. First if there was any glass such as in a museum. When a flash reflects off glass, it can create a ghostly glow. Also, someone else standing near may be caught in a reflection so I take into consideration if anyone else was around. I make sure there was no artificial light, such as headlights from passing cars or flashlights. If the picture is taken outdoors, there can be bugs that can create a streak of light across the picture if caught just right and animals can create bizarre shadows as well as ghostly glowing eyes. Many things can be contaminating to spirit photography so it is important to recognize these things, because practice makes perfect.

I'm not saying it is impossible to catch a ghost on film but it is rare. Some people go years without capturing anything worth consideration. Ghost hunting takes patience and perseverance. Take as many pictures as you can even if it is purposefully with the above-mentioned contamination factors. This will help you to know exactly what you are looking for and what to dismiss.

Ghosts of 1600

When we hear the address 1600 Pennsylvania Avenue, we think of the beautiful historic White House in Washington D.C. Construction first began in 1792 but it wasn't until November 1800 that the house had its first occupants, President John Adams and his wife Abigail. Since then this grand building has been the home to our country's presidents and like any other home has seen its share of intense emotions and unforgettable events. As I've previously discussed, whenever there is that much emotion and history tied to a location it creates a perfect breeding ground for paranormal activity.

Lincoln's Ghost

The most common reports of a ghost in the White house are that of our 16th president Abraham Lincoln. Mr. Lincoln served as President from 1861 to 1865 when he was assassinated at Ford's Theatre. During his term, it has been reported that he and his wife would hold séances in the Green Room in attempts to contact their deceased son. There is also the report that President Lincoln had a dream of his own death, hearing people sob and seeing a casket, he asked a guard who had died and was told the President. These reports indicate that Mr. Lincoln was a very "mystical" man but was it his belief in spirits or the fact that he led our country during the traumatic Civil War that has made his spirit remain at the White House.

Grace Coolidge, wife of Calvin Coolidge, was one of the first to report seeing the apparition of President Lincoln standing in the Oval Office with hands clasped behind his back, looking out. There have been other reports of seeing the ghost of the former President, usually a knock on the door to those who stay in or near his former bedroom, some will see his image and it will slowly fade, others have seen him pacing and agitated in the second-floor hallway. Yet Mr. Lincoln is not the only ghostly apparition at the White House.

First Lady Apparitions

Dolly Madison, who planted the beautiful rose garden on the White House grounds, has been said to appear there and it has even been reported that she stopped an attempt made to dig up the garden by First Lady Ellen Wilson 100 years later. No one has attempted to disturb the garden since.

Abigail Adams' ghost has been seen in the East Room hanging laundry to dry, since at the time of her residency construction had not been completed, this was the warmest and driest room in the house.

Black Cats and Restless Spirits

Andrew Jackson is believed to still occupy the Rose Room, where his bed can still be found. Mary Todd Lincoln was said to have heard Mr. Jackson making noise and cursing.

Another interesting report is that of Anne Surratt. Her mother Mary was executed on July 7, 1865 for her involvement with the assassination of President Lincoln. Anne is believed to appear on the steps of the White House on the anniversary of her mom's death still pleading for her release.

On a more bizarre note, there have been reports of a black "demon cat" in the White House basement. This cat is believed only to appear at night and only when someone is alone. Initially the feline will appear as a helpless kitten, but upon moving closer it will increase in size and its demeanor will take a dark turn. This cat is said to be a bad omen. Reports of seeing the "demon cat" always occur before a tragic event. One of the first reports of the cat occurred before the great stock market crash in 1929 and it was also seen before the assassination of JFK.

In 1952, there was reconstructive work done at the White House and the reports of paranormal activity, though still occurring, have decreased. There has always been great curiosity about what takes place behind those grand doors. This has been a place of great victory, defeat, joy, sorrow, mystery, and intrigue. There is no doubt that the energy in this building will continue to surge and those who loved to stay may continue to stay, those who feel they have unfinished business may continue to work, and those who need the inspiration of great former Leaders and First Ladies may find it when it is least expected.

Haunted Works of Art

Have you ever seen a painting that just gave you an uneasy feeling, or perhaps felt the eyes of a portrait following you? Is it possible that a simple work of art could be haunted? Art is made to stir emotion. Some images stay with us or remind us of evil or darkness. Simple images can "haunt" a person's mind, but can something within the painting itself be paranormal? An artist will put much of themselves into a painting and at times can capture the essence of another in a portrait, but can this act stir up more than just hidden emotions? Here are some examples of art pieces believed to have a supernatural touch to them.

Madame Delphine Lalaurie

A New Orleans Mardi Gras painter named Ricardo Pustanio was asked by a resident of the Lalaurie home to paint a portrait of the former socialite. She became infamous during the 1830s not only for her high stature in social circles but also because of her involvement with the torture of slaves. The painting was done in 2003 using whatever images the painter could find. The resident hung the painting; quite pleased by the response visitors would give, some even assuming the painting was an original part of the home that was believed to be haunted. Séances were held as well for tourists and paranormal researchers and they would watch in astonishment as the painting would rock or fall from the wall. Soon the resident claimed frightening things were happening due to this painting so he gave it to another tenant. Soon the new owner of the painting returned it to the artist. She claimed the eyes would follow her, the expression would change, and that she heard it sigh. The painting is now with a private collection and it is unknown if the new owners have experienced anything that was described by the first two.

The Crying Boy

In the early 1980's the British tabloid The Sun released a story of several house fires occurring in a short period of time. There was one strange thing these homes had in common, each contained a painting of a young boy shedding a tear, and these paintings were always untouched by the flames. Once the story was published, there were several calls from people who owned the print stating that they too had suffered fires. Several weeks later, the paper encouraged everyone to send in their copies of The Crying Boy to be destroyed and end the "curse". One woman claimed to try to set fires to 2 copies of the painting but to her horror, they would not burn. The origin behind the painting is just as mysterious. Some theories are that the boy was an orphan whose parents died in a fire; another is of the painter taking in the young boy only to have his studio burn. There have also been psychics who have studied the painting and reported the child is stuck inside the print. There are several variations of this painting; the boy's age and clothing differ slightly. There have been reports as recent as early 2000 of fires occurring with this painting in the home, some are still dismissing the story as nothing more than an urban legend.

Pogo the Clown

John Wayne Gacy was executed in 1994 for several murders, yet his alter ego is still causing trauma. Gacy once performed as Pogo the Clown at children's parties. As an artist, he would often paint images of Pogo. These paintings were sought after. Soon the people who possessed these works of art were seeking to get rid of them, due to tragic events occurring. These events would range from what seemed like a streak of bad luck, to more serious events such as car crashes and suicides.

Hands Resist Him aka Haunted eBay Painting

Bill Stoneham painted hands Resist Him in 1972. The painting shows Bill as a young boy standing in front of a dark glass door with several hands appearing behind him. At his side is a doll like girl with a very disturbing expression on her face. The glass was said to be the veil between waking and dreaming, the little girl is the guide between the two realms, and the hands represented other lives.

Both the owner of the Gallery where the painting was displayed and the critic who reviewed the showing passed away within a year of the show. No one is sure how the painting became abandoned but it showed up on eBay in February of 2000 with the title of "Haunted Painting".

The disclaimer that followed reports that the seller found it and brought it home feeling it was a good piece of art. Later their young daughter claimed the two children in the painting were fighting and coming into her room at night. A motion camera was set up and it is said the young boy seemed to appear as if he were coming out of the painting. Soon they decided the artwork had to go and warned potential buyers not to bid if they suffered from heart or nervous conditions. Some are even afraid to view the painting.

The last bid on "Hands" was for $1,025.00 and the work of art eventually had a new owner. An interview with the new owner in March 2000 stated that they had not had any experiences themselves but received several emails from people wondering how they can live with such a thing in their home. Suggestions on how to cleanse the home were also received as well as warnings never to let young children view the painting. This was the last known owner and though it was stated they would eventually sell the painting, the auction has been closed since early 2000.

So, is it possible that such things exist? Can the soul of another be caught in a painting? True art comes from within, and it may be very possible to have that connection between our planes of existence and beyond caught on canvas. The next time a painting gives you the creeps, try researching the artist and the subject. Quite a few pieces of art out there carry more of a supernatural quality than one may think.

Haunting Profits

How much would you pay to experience a haunting? Some may ask why anyone would want to expose themselves to spirits intentionally. Others who are interested in ghost hunting feel this is a good way to start out in the field. While there are tours and events at reportedly haunted locations all over the U.S and abroad, some want a more personal experience. This is where "haunted" auction items come into play.

Haunted Dolls

There are some famous stories of haunted items picked up at auctions, like "The haunted eBay painting" that I discussed in a previous article. Some paranormal enthusiasts may be familiar with Harold, believed to be one of the first "haunted" dolls sold online. Harold was very active, moving on its own and voices were heard coming from the doll. A woman bought Harold who intended to use the doll as practice for restorations, but she had what seemed to be several incidents of "bad luck" once the doll was in her possession. This bad luck included physical harm and even the deaths of people close to her. She put Harold back up for auction with the warning he was cursed. Harold now has a new owner and even his own website that tells his story and documents his activity. There is an even more bizarre story of a lady who bought a "cursed voodoo doll" online. She ignored the warnings to not take the doll out of its packaging and put it up for display. Once the doll attacked her, she tried to destroy it but nothing worked. She tried to ship the doll back but it always came right back to her doorstep. Not everyone she sought help from, including paranormal teams, could help her so the doll is now locked away in her attic.

Authenticity?

Since coming across these stories, it seems there are now hundreds, possibly more, of objects up at online auctions with claims of being haunted. If you are planning to look for such a thing to start out in paranormal investigation, here are a few things to keep in mind.

The choice in words that are used when describing the object is crucial. I have seen stones or jewels up for auction with claims that they are haunted or possessed by Wiccan or Pagan magic. Keep in mind items like these are "charged" during certain spells or rituals. Energy used in magic and spirit energy, though seemingly similar, are different. Always read the description carefully, sometimes there are inconsistencies such as time frame and type of activity. Sometimes people are caught up in telling a good story over facts.

Observe the photos carefully. I have seen so many dolls up for auction that have obviously been tampered with to look scary, paint splotches that resemble blood or "strange symbols" drawn on the dolls clothing. Clowns and ventriloquist dummies are also popular because they naturally have a "creepy" appearance to them.

Make sure you aren't taken advantage of. If an object is really causing terror in someone's life, they will more than likely want to get rid of it at a reasonable price. I have seen objects starting at nearly nothing while others can sell for over one thousand dollars.

Research as much as you can about what you're buying. The seller should be willing to answer questions about the object. If you feel you don't have enough information then move on. There are objects with claims they were used in "dark rituals" or Voodoo ceremonies, when in fact the seller is just using terms that are naturally not received well by society to hit the fear trigger.

Mind Over Matter?

Always keep in mind the power of suggestion is always possible. If you read a long entry about an object's activity such as a doll moving on its own you will keep that in mind and may want to see the activity so much your mind can play tricks on you. I am certainly not saying there is no such thing as a haunted object, I have seen many, but go into being the new owner with an open mind. Try to collect photo, video, or audio evidence to share.

The last warning, consider what you're bringing into your home. Just because you are interested in having a haunted object doesn't mean everyone in the home is just as enthusiastic. True, haunted objects may not always "perform" for everyone and someone who does not wish to be involved may be the recipient or witness of the activity.

Improve Your Chances of Spirit Communication

So, you want to be a ghost hunter. You have picked your location and of course have permission to investigate the area. You have done your research on the history of the location, such as who lived or worked there and if they passed on, you know how it happened. You have extensive notes on the type of activity reported and the camera, flashlights and digital recorder are ready. However, none of this will guarantee you will experience an encounter. Many times, investigators come up empty handed; it takes time, patience and persistence. So how do you improve your chances of experiencing paranormal activity?

Type of Haunting

You may not be aware if the activity is residual or intelligent until you get started. Once you have done your research it is a good idea to bring a few "props" with you to aid in the communication process. For example, if the reports are of the ghost of a child you may want to bring a few toys with you and attempt to coax the child into playing. Leave the toys behind and return later to see if anything has been moved or altered in any way. Young spirits are often shy and hide. Another example would be if you know the spirit is of a person who liked to play poker, bring a set of cards with you and sit down to a game as if you know someone is joining you. Make sure you have the digital recorder and cameras ready.

Toolkit

Certain tools can also be used to detect immediate responses. If the spirit is strong enough it can make the temperature in the room drop or rise and if you have an EMF detector it can come in handy. Spirits pull energy in order to manifest and this will affect the temperature as well as the surrounding electromagnetic field. If these tools are not available to you, there are easier techniques. Try to loosen the bottom of your flashlight enough so that it takes a slight touch to bring the light back on. Lay the flashlight down on a steady surface and begin communicating. Explain that if they touch the flashlight and make it come on, that is a yes answer. Be patient, remember some spirits are from a time so long ago that this is all new technology; it may take a moment for the spirit understand. A simple call bell works as well, one ring for yes and two for no.

Communicate

How you communicate is also crucial. At times, the spirit does not realize they are no longer part of the living world. Try speaking to them as if you are part of their old life. If they were once a nurse, try speaking to them as if you're a patient in need. Were they involved in an old war? If so, try speaking about the battle they were a part of as if it is still occurring. Another point to keep in mind is the possibility there may be a language barrier depending on the location.

There may come a time when the spirit is angry or had a violent past. Take great caution with how you approach these situations. For example, if they were a former prisoner, you may want to act as though you are on their side instead of one of the prison guards. Provoking is another popular technique but not always recommended. Sometimes, the investigator is so caught up in trying to get evidence that they will become aggressive with the entity, calling it a coward or challenging it to do something to prove its existence. There have been reports of spirits scratching, biting or even physically pushing investigators. Do not risk your safety for the sake of proof.

Stay Calm and Quiet

One of the most common mistakes occurs when you do finally make contact. It can be very exciting if the spirit is able to play, ring the bell, or turn on the light but don't stop the session there. Continue asking important questions for as long as possible. The energy the spirit uses to manifest can be very short lived so time is everything, use it wisely. If you hear a noise, remain quiet to try to determine the source and direction, you may want to communicate with fellow investigators right away but try to refrain until the activity has ceased. You may want to use hand gestures to ask if they heard or witnessed the same things.

Even with all these tricks, you may still go away empty handed. If it is a residual haunting it is not going to be able to communicate because it is simply like a silent movie playing over and over, unaware of your presence. Spirits that are part of an intelligent haunting are what we all hope to connect with, to get evidence, gain knowledge, and even help the ghost move on. This takes time, so if the first session is not a success simply try again.

In The Shadows

We've all had it happen, you see a dark shadow from the corner of your eye, but as soon as you turn to look at it straight on, it's gone. Almost as if it dove out of sight on purpose, but how could that be? There is an even more alarming experience. Something startles you awake in the middle of the night, you see a dark shadow standing at the foot of the bed, watching you. This has to be a trick of the light or maybe you're not fully awake and your eyes need to adjust, right? Not necessarily.

Shadow Beings

There have been numerous reports of these shadow beings, also called shadow people or shadow men. Even more numerous are the theories regarding their intentions for visiting us. Sightings differ; some witness a thin wispy shadow, barely holding a form that seems to float away quickly, into the darkness. Some even seem to go through walls or up into the ceiling. These appear to be the most common sightings. They seem to avoid contact at all costs and are not happy about being spotted.

Another type that is commonly seen is much more confident. They are human-like in form and usually appear as males, yet they do not seem to hide so quickly. Some have reported coming face to face, or shall I say "faceless", with them or seeing them standing very still in the corner of a room, barely noticeable at first. Then you see it, this shadow is much darker than any other shadow in the room. There have been sightings of a much more sinister type of shadow being, usually appearing in a fedora type hat or even a cloak at times. Some have even said they've witnessed glowing red or green eyes, or no eyes at all just vacant black holes.

Who Are They?

So many different types of these beings, but what are they? Once again, theories abound. The most common is these beings are from another dimension and come in and out to simply learn and observe. Another very common suspicion is that these are a type of alien visiting from another planet, but again just to watch, as if we were their own personal reality show. Less talked about is the theory that these beings may be the result of someone else's astral projection trip. If someone does manage to have an out of body experience, would their astral body appear as a dark faceless shadow? The more sinister "hat man" or "cloaked" beings have been called demons, or even omens, warning someone that they are of ill health or about to pass on, especially since the cloaked form resembles a grim reaper. Even the size of the shadow can differ, usually from three feet to six feet, and how often they appear can vary. Some people will see them almost daily for a few years and then not at all. Children may see them often but then never see them as adults.

Encounters

When they choose not to ignore you, the actual encounters are rare but leave a lasting impression, people report feeling frightened and drained of energy, as if the being is absorbing your emotions into themselves. If touched, these shadow entities can feel like pure electricity or several degrees colder. The rare malicious ones will try to intimidate the "victim" making them feel as if they are surrounded by darkness, suffocating, or even produce brief paralysis such as Old Hag Syndrome. Bite wounds and scratches have been reported in these attacks but so few of them have occurred or have been brought to the public's attention. One of my favorite explanations is these shadow people are a type of "men in black" who appear after a UFO or alien sighting to intimidate the witness to forget what they saw.

Whatever they are, they have been a huge topic of conversation in the paranormal community. Very few have been photographed and though they are human-like, but not human or known to vocalize, EVPs cannot be taken. I hope that more solid information will be available one day, we can learn just as much from them as they can from us.

Just Add Water

Water has long been described as so many things; it has been a symbol of cleansing and purification, a source needed to sustain life, and a home to many forms of plants and animals. However, many bodies of water are also home to spirits as well.

The Flying Dutchman

Many have heard of The Flying Dutchman. In 1680, a ship captained by a man named Hendrick Vanderdecken, set sail from Amsterdam to Batavia. A terrible storm was approaching as they came to the Cape of Good Hope and the crew believed it to be a sign from God. The captain ignored all warnings and continued. The storm claimed the ship and its passengers. Now, there is the belief that Vanderdecken and his crew are forced to roam the waters near the cape for eternity as punishment.

There have been many sightings of The Flying Dutchman; the first recorded sighting was in 1835 by a British ship. The crew saw the phantom ship approaching during a storm, it came so close the crew feared they would collide but the ship disappeared. The last recorded sighting was in 1942 by four witnesses off the coast of Cape Town. They reported seeing the ship sail into Table Bay and vanish.

Cursed Ship

So now that we have covered a well-known ghost ship, how about the story of a ship that many believed to be cursed? Christened in 1861, the Amazon seemed to be the epitome of "bad luck". Just 48 hours after taking command of the ship, its captain died suddenly. When she finally had her maiden voyage, the ship struck a fishing dam leaving a large gash in the hull. While this damage was being repaired, a fire broke out. Soon the ship was operational again but during only the third time crossing the Atlantic, The Amazon collided with another ship. In 1867, the ship was wrecked and abandoned off the coast of Newfoundland. Someone decided to put faith back into her because it was raised and restored by an American company who sailed south to sell the ship. In 1872, Captain Benjamin Briggs purchased the Amazon and renamed her Mary Celeste. Captain Briggs raised the sails and with his family headed toward the Mediterranean. The story doesn't end there. In December of 1872, the crew of the Dei Gratia found the Mary Celeste floating, completely unattended, about 600 miles off the coast of Portugal. Nothing appeared to be wrong, the ship was in perfect condition, the sails were set and the cargo had not been touched. The crew's belongings were still on board and a breakfast sat as if someone had started but never finished it. There was no sign of a storm or a struggle and the last entry to the log was made On November 24th. The entry did not describe any trouble or hardship. If the ship was abandoned shortly after the last entry, it would have been drifting for a week and a half but according to the crew of the Dei Gratia, this was not possible due to the way the ship's sails were set and its location. The ship was guided for several days after the last entry, yet Captain Briggs, his family and crew were never found.

Haunted Waters

Phantom ships, cursed ships, all part of the mysterious seas, but what about the water itself being haunted? In 1924 crewmembers of the S.S Watertown, James Courtney and Michael Meehan, were cleaning a cargo tank when both were overcome by gas fumes and died. The custom at the time was to bury the sailors at sea. For several days after their burial, the two men's faces were seen in the water following the ship. The Captain reported the strange occurrence to his employees and it was suggested he try to photograph the images. He did just that and the photo is quite eerie. Two ghostly faces can be seen as if they are rising from the water itself. However, the photo's authenticity has been debated for decades.

There is no denying; tales of the haunted seas have been very popular for centuries. They bring about images of pirates, hidden treasures, and glorious ships. There are still things we have yet to discover lurking in the deep waters, and there are still things shrouded in aquatic mystery that have yet to discover us.

Need A Lift?

Imagine this; you are driving down the road on a foggy or rainy night when you come to the entrance of a bridge that crosses a river. Near the entrance, you see a woman who is obviously in distress on the side of the road. You pull over and offer your assistance which she gratefully accepts. The woman gets into your car and tells you she is attempting to get to her mother's house and gives you an address. While you drive over the bridge, you engage in a nice conversation with her until you notice she has become very silent. Soon you realize you are over the bridge and your passenger has disappeared. This is just one story of Phantom Hitchhikers. This case takes place in Columbia South Carolina at US-76, but there are accounts all over the world.

Phantom Passengers

These stories are very popular, probably because they involve actual interaction with a spirit. You are not just seeing a ghost but it is talking with or responding to you. There are different types of these tales. Most common are the stories as the one we just spoke of, a person is driving and sees a person on the side of the road in either distress or just hitching a ride. They get into the car and give a destination. Sometimes the destination is where they met their end or in other tales, it could be the cemetery in which they're buried. The most common understanding of the phenomenon is the person does not realize they have passed and are still attempting to reach their destination.

Look Out

Another example is a much more dangerous one. In Hong Kong, there is Tuen Mun Road. This is one of the main roads and is heavily used. There have been several reports of ghosts walking, or simply appearing, in the middle of the road. Drivers then quickly swerve out of the way to avoid hitting what they think is a living person and cause serious if not fatal accidents. There is a theory that the number of apparitions are growing due to the number of fatal accidents that keep occurring.

Out of Harm's Way

The third example, takes place in San Antonio Texas. This case has been labeled an urban legend. Some have even argued that there is a scientific explanation, but let's concentrate on the paranormal aspect for now shall we? Near the San Juan Mission, there is an intersection that is crossed by train tracks. The story states that sometime in the 1930s or 40's a school bus filled with children stalled on these tracks. Despite the driver's efforts, the quickly approaching train collided with the bus, killing 10 children. Today it is believed these children are still near the tracks, protecting other drivers from stalling and meeting the same fate. They say if you park on the tracks, then put your car in neutral and wait, the car will be pushed forward out of the way of the tracks. In addition, if you put powder on the bumper beforehand, you will see small childlike handprints once the car is out of harm's way. As stated before this is more of an urban legend since there is no official record of this accident but it doesn't stop people from attempting to stop on the tracks. There have been many examples of ghosts appearing to warn drivers of dangerous road conditions. Usually the entity had passed from a similar hazard, and now they are protecting you from a similar fate. These entities have even been labeled as guardian angels.

The road can be a dangerous place. It is always important to be alert and focused while driving, for your own safety and the safety of others. Always keep your eyes on the road and if you come across any hitchhikers, you may want to remember a few of these tales. There are several books and articles that list some reportedly haunted roads, you may want to do a little research before taking a road trip or offering a ride to a stranger in need. However, there are some, like myself, who would enjoy the company of a phantom hitchhiker.

Non-Human Entities

When we think of the paranormal, we usually think of spirits of those who have passed on. We think of cold spots, barely visible forms, and disembodied voices. Yet a lot of us automatically think we are dealing with human entities. There are a number of non-human entities that are part of the paranormal world. Here I will briefly discuss a few. This is such a broad topic and depending on religion and culture, these entities can vary greatly but there are some similarities that I will highlight.

Angels

These entities have a similar appearance throughout many cultures and religions. People are believed to have encounters with angels during times of trauma. Many describe a feeling of calm and comfort. Some feel they are enveloped with warmth or see a bright glow and what appears to be a human with wings. The entity is usually unfamiliar, unlike those who see or hear from a deceased family member or friend. Angels are believed to be protectors and at times may deliver important messages. Many feel they have a Guardian Angel who stays with them throughout their life to guide and offer protection from harm. Another common theory on angels is that they were never human to begin with. They are from a "higher power" or "divine being" and there is an ongoing debate if these entities have free will. There is also the theory that angels are simply an extension of our subconscious as a way of communicating with our own "higher self".

Demons

Known to be more negative than the above-mentioned entity, there are a few theories of what demons actually are. Some feel demons are merely fallen angels; others feel they are a form of an elemental that is described below. Similarities among different cultures are that these entities are never pleasant. Demons are usually brought forth from another plane by either summoning or the demon may be attached to a certain person or place. There have been reports of the smell of sulfur in the area when a demon is present or a feeling of heaviness on the chest. Also, there is a rule among paranormal investigators never to, under any circumstances, use a provoking method when dealing with a demonic entity. These entities have been known to leave scratches or even bite marks when confronted or angered. Reports of actually seeing a demon are rare but their physical appearance is generally the same among different cultures and religions. They are usually described as human-like, possibly with animal or goat-like legs or feet, shorter in stature with twisted or disproportionate facial features.

Elementals

A type of Nature spirit, Elementals are believed to embody the elements of earth, air, fire, and water. These spirits are usually encountered during spell work and some believe they can communicate with Elementals through their dreams. Common Elementals known throughout the world are gnomes, sprites and faeries just to name a few. There are numerous names, forms, and purposes for these entities but they are universally known as those who keep balance among nature. As I mentioned above, some feel demons are a type of elemental since there is no defining personality of these spirits, some are described as kind and helpful, some mischievous and some angry or envious of the mortal world.

Animal Spirits

Just as many believe they have a guardian angel to watch and protect them, there is also the belief in animal spirits or totems. These spirits are a very personal and deep connection to one's inner-self. As mentioned above, many use spell work to communicate with these spirits. Another way to encounter these entities is through meditation. There are many books written on ways to find your own personal animal spirit. These entities can appear as messengers with warnings or to protect us from harm. Modern culture is filled with stories of crows being associated with death, cats associated with witches, or a serpent associated with evil. These animals have all had significance in many different parts of the world. Some may not even know the origin of such labels but there is almost a universal understanding of the symbolism such as the owl for wisdom, the horse for power, or the vulture for a scavenger. These animals have held these roles in the spirit world as well.

These are just a few examples of the many different entities besides human ghosts that make up the wide realm of the paranormal.

Paranormal Activity Vs Haunting

Very often the term Paranormal Activity seems to go hand in hand with ghosts and haunting, however the term means so much more than this. Especially with the popular movies, the word paranormal is everywhere now. What does this mean and why is it different from a haunting?

Paranormal or Bad Wiring

The word paranormal means anything that cannot be explained by science. Many times, someone may feel their home is haunted due to unexplained phenomena occurring. Commonly you'll hear someone describe their lights flickering, or a feeling of being watched when they enter a certain room. Upon proper investigation, one may discover that the home is not haunted and these experiences are not paranormal. One common tool is an EMF detector. This tool measures electromagnetic fields. A high EMF reading can occur for many reasons, if you are near an electrical source such as an outlet, certain wiring or even types of plumbing can give a high EMF reading. Severely high readings can cause physical effects on a person such as dizziness, nausea, and even a feeling of paranoia. If it is revealed that there is faulty or very old wiring in a home this can explain the flickering lights and an uneasy feeling. These things are explained by science and therefore not paranormal. Nonetheless, if you receive a high reading and these issues are not a factor, or the reading spikes from very high to normal, and you are nowhere near an electrical source, then this is unexplained and therefore it is paranormal.

Other examples of the paranormal include extraterrestrial activity, poltergeists activity, telekinesis, and even astral projection can be described as paranormal.

Though there are many theories, science has neither proven nor disproven these things. I however believe in it all but this still does not make it a scientific fact.

Haunting?

Now let's look at another example. When someone moves into a new home and is informed the previous owner passed away in that house, they may have an uneasy feeling to begin with but decide to move in anyway. Soon they realize certain objects keep disappearing, and then reappearing in different locations. A first thought would be the ghost of the previous owner is making itself known, however no apparition has been seen. These occurrences cannot be labeled, just yet, as a haunting; they are simply paranormal. Soon, along with this paranormal activity, our new homeowner awakens to the sight of an elderly woman making her way down the hallway, she is almost transparent, and seems to be gliding just above the floor. Well this must have been just a bizarre dream. The next morning someone else in the family describes seeing the same strange woman. Soon she continues to appear, now we can say that this house is haunted. A haunting is the habitual visitation of a ghost or apparition.

As I discussed in a previous article-haunting can be residual, meaning the spirit has no idea you are there, it isn't aware of surroundings or changes, it is more of an imprint from a certain time. Imagine a movie playing repeatedly, the same routine, the same motions, just repeating. The haunting can also be intelligent, meaning the spirit is aware of you and able to interact or communicate. Without the spirit, there is no haunting, just paranormal occurrences.

Even though ghosts themselves cannot be explained by science, it is the act of their frequent appearance that defines a haunting. There will always be debate about what a ghost is and even deeper; what are the exact contents of a soul, and if or how is it left behind, just as many artists describe being haunted by music, scents, or words. These, of course are just symbols, giving a figurative spirit to such things and describing the frequent visitation of the uninvited. I suppose you could be haunted by just about anything.

Phone Calls from the Dead

The Chatsworth crash took place in California's San Fernando Valley on September 12, 2008 when a commuter train collided with a freight train. This unfortunate event claimed the lives of 25 people, one of which was a 49-year-old man named Charles E Peck who was headed to a job interview.

One Last Call

Peck's fiancé and other family members were on their way to pick him up when they heard about the crash on the radio. His family kept hope that he had survived the crash due to several calls from his cell phone. Peck's fiancé, brother, sister, son and stepmother all received a total of 35 calls over 11 hours but whenever they would answer there would be nothing but static on the other end. When the family tried returning the calls, they would go straight to voicemail.

The numerous calls prompted the search team to trace the signal and search the remains of the first train. One hour after the last call was received from Peck's cell phone, his deceased body was discovered and it was confirmed that he had died upon impact, his cell phone was never found.

Can You Hear Me?

Was it possible that Charles Peck had attempted to reach his loved ones after his passing? This phenomenon occurs quite often. Many people claim to receive calls from deceased loved ones. Usually these calls occur a few hours after the person has passed but there have been occurrences even several years later. The people who receive these calls are not necessarily believers in the paranormal nor are they looking for a supernatural experience.

The similarities reported with these calls are that the voices, though recognizable, seem very distant and are often diluted by static. The caller ID will normally show as "private" or all zeros. Those that receive the calls may only hear a brief message or at times have a short conversation and may not hear a dial tone when the call is disconnected. There have even been reports of text messages received from the deceased. Some believe these calls are an example of EVP or electronic voice phenomenon.

The purpose of these calls also varies. Some report hearing a reassuring message letting them know everything will be ok and that they are loved. There have also been reports of these calls being received on a birthday or anniversary. In some even stranger cases, are reports of calls being received with a warning from the deceased, such as an unknown illness in the family that should be checked or a suggested change in travel plans, maybe to avoid a potential fatal accident?

But...How?

How and why does this happen? There are many theories. One theory among the paranormal community is the knowledge that spirits can manipulate and pull energy. If a spirit can use this energy to manifest or move objects why not phone lines? Skeptics believe that the calls are hallucinations of grieving family members.

Everyone has, at least once, asked themselves what happens after we pass from this life. Whatever your beliefs are, we all just want the comfort of being told everything will be all right. So maybe, just maybe, our loved ones, through pure energy and emotion, will find a way to deliver that and other important messages when we need them the most.

Poltergeists

The word poltergeist comes from the German word poltern meaning rumble or noise and geist meaning ghost or spirit. These noisy spirits are known to cause trouble. They are characterized by their ability to move stationary objects such as furniture. Some people may report hearing knocking or scratching sounds. They have even been known to write notes and, at times, cause physical harm by hitting or slapping whoever occupies the "haunted" location. There are rare reports of actually seeing the source of the poltergeist activity and there are two main theories of why and how this activity occurs.

Entity or Self-Induced?

The first theory is that it is a ghost that has such a high level of energy it is able to move objects, cause noises, and make themselves known. The other theory is that this is an example of psychokinesis, or the ability to move objects generated by energy in the brain. This raises the debate whether poltergeists are really a paranormal occurrence or not. Below are two cases, one example of the activity being caused by a spirit's high energy and another that discusses the high emotional state of a human as the source of the activity.

Case #1; Danny

Al Cobb from Savannah Georgia bought a vintage 1800s bed as a present for his teenage son Jason. After about three nights, Jason reported feeling as if someone were leaning on the pillow, watching him and that he could feel a cold breath. The next night he noticed a picture of his grandparents turned face down, Jason sat the photo upright and the next morning the photo was moved once again. Later in the day, after returning to the room Jason noticed several toys moved to the center of the bed. Finally, his parents began to take notice. Al decided to ask if there was a ghost present to reveal its name and age. He then left a piece of lined paper and a crayon on the bed. The family returned several minutes later to find written on the paper in a child's script the word Danny and the number seven. Al encouraged the communication with the spirit and Danny continued to leave notes. Danny explained that his mother had passed away in that bed in 1899 and he wanted to stay there with it; he also left a note warning "no one sleep in bed". Jason had moved out of the room but stretched out on the bed one day possibly to test that warning, and upon getting up a piece of wall décor flew across the room, barely missing him. A spirit seemed to reveal itself as the source of the occurrences around the bed yet a parapsychologist who studied the case argues it was the electromagnetic energy of the wall that the bed was moved to that caused a heightened psychic ability in Jason.

Case #2; Macomb

In 1948 in Macomb, Illinois, a teenage girl named Wanet Macneill was forced to move with her father to her uncle's farm after her parent's bitter divorce. Wanet was very emotionally disturbed and her emotions ran high. Soon small fires began erupting all over the farm. They began as small brown spots on the wallpaper and would soon burst into flames. This would happen day after day and the family began to keep pans and buckets around the house so water was readily available to extinguish the fires. Neighbors would come to assist and witness the phenomena. The fire chief was even called and decided to strip all of the wallpaper. Soon they witnessed the brown spots appear on the bare wall and then burst into flames. The fires began to ignite in several other rooms as well as the porch. In one week, over 200 fires broke out and finally claimed the entire house. Other areas of the farm including the barn began to suffer the same fate. The fire marshal questioned Wanet and came to the conclusion that she was starting the fires with matches when no one was looking, which pleased the authorities, but several witnesses refused to believe this since they had witnessed the fires erupt without any form of heat or fire such as a match. Many believed that because Wanet was so unhappy with the living situation, she was causing the fires with the kinetic energy of her mind.

There will always be the debate if this activity is spiritual or scientific. There are several reported cases and the source is always controversial. Yet this activity will always remain in a category of its own due to the intensity of the cases and the emotions involved.

Residual Haunting VS Intelligent Haunting

There are quite a few different types of hauntings, but I wanted to discuss two that are often misunderstood by those who are not in the field of paranormal research. Let's look into the differences between a residual haunting and an intelligent haunting.

Residual Haunting

A residual haunting can be best described as a recording, a moment in time that will continue to play out repeatedly. For example, a person dealing with a residual haunting may mention they notice the same sound of a woman crying or the same smell of a cigar at a specific time every day. Nothing ever changes with this activity and some believe that these are not even spirits but imprints in time. With a residual haunting, there is no way to interact during an investigation. Even if a full-bodied apparition is seen with this activity, it is not aware of our presence. What causes a residual haunting is still up for debate, but a common theory is that it is left over energy that has somehow become part of the surrounding area. A very important, life changing, or traumatic event that was so significant it is now timeless and runs on a continuous loop.

Intelligent Haunting

An intelligent haunting is one with which we can interact. This involves a spirit or entity that can somehow communicate with us as we ask questions or request actions. This type of haunting does not follow a specific pattern or routine. This may be a spirit of a human who had a sudden or traumatic death and may not realize they have passed away, or in some extreme cases, a non-human entity. While investigating an intelligent haunting is rewarding to experience, it does not offer a guarantee. The spirit or entity may not always be cooperative or friendly. There is more of a risk when investigating an intelligent haunting.

Stay Focused

As always, timing is everything. While doing an investigation always research what type of haunting is taking place. A residual haunting can occur at the same time every day, a few times a month or just on a specific anniversary once a year. An intelligent haunting is something that occurs more randomly. During any investigation, it is important to keep all of your senses sharp. When investigating an intelligent haunting make sure you are aware of the spirit activity involved, whether it is human, non-human, passive, or aggressive. This will not only help to keep you safe but also allows for the best preparation.

If you can experience either type of haunting you are very lucky. To experience a residual haunting, you have the chance to witness something so intense it was permanently absorbed into and continues to bleed through time itself. To experience an intelligent haunting, you have the ability to attempt contact and receive answers to age-old questions of the afterlife. Paranormal investigating equipment is improving rapidly which enables us to acquire the proof we so desperately need, and to continue our education involving the paranormal.

Are Talking Boards "Just Toys"?

Talking Boards, also known as Witch Boards, or more commonly Ouija Boards, have always been a controversial subject among almost everyone. Can these boards really be used to communicate with the other side, and if so, why are many of these boards sold through toy stores as "games" or novelty items? How did such things end up being marketed to young children and teens who are often inexperienced with the paranormal? In fact, many people credit their first paranormal experience to the use of these boards. A few of these questions are answered in the history of the Talking Board.

Early Spirit Communication

The Ouija board was not the first tool used in an attempt to communicate with spirits. In fact, the Planchette, the object used to point to the letters and numbers on these boards, was once used all by itself. The word Planchette translates to "Little Plank" in French and was once used with pencils attached to the legs by mediums for automatic writing. The idea behind automatic writing was to have the spirit "take over" the medium and write out messages for friends or family that eagerly awaited answers or just simply needed closure.

The Beginning of the Ouija

The actual board came from E.C. Reiche, a cabinet and coffin maker from Maryland who made a wooden tray with letters and numbers. The Planchette was then modified to be used without the pencils so it could be moved easily around the board. The word Ouija comes from combining the French and German words for "yes", oui and ja. Reiche later sold the invention to Charles Kennard who founded the Kennard Novelty Company. He and William H. A. Maupin filed for the first patent on these boards on May 28, 1890. This is where the better-known name Ouija comes into use, William Fuld, who was the shop manager at the time, decided to go into business for himself and changed the name to the Ouija Novelty Company. This company was later sold to Parker Brothers© in 1966. This is how the boards ended up in toy store aisles.

A "Fun Toy"

Today these boards come in many different styles with the same basic idea, there is even a pink Ouija board made especially for girls, but the question remains, is this really something to "play" with? There are hundreds of cautionary tales about using these boards. We have all heard the stories of one being used at a teen party for fun, and then weird things begin to happen. The candles that were lit are blown out, there are scratching sounds on the wall, whispering noises and so on. Some believe these boards are an easy way to open a gateway. You are not only openly inviting spirits into your home but also allowing it to manipulate your own movements by guiding the planchette to reveal messages. There is even the belief that those using these boards open themselves up for possession by demons or inhuman entities, that once a gateway is opened there is no guarantee of who or what you're getting. Another theory is the board is a simple divination tool like tarot cards or the pendulum, our subconscious is really the one guiding the planchette to the letters or numbers and there is no spirit involvement what so ever.

An Ongoing Trend

The answer may never be completely clear about how the board works, but the one thing most agree on is the mystery surrounding it is what has kept it selling for well over a century. There are books on Ouija, collectors of Ouija, and even an online Ouija board! This little invention is everywhere and in many forms. We will continue to see them make appearances at parties and in movies as long as there are people who are intrigued by the unknown and enjoy feeling a little scared, after all, it's just a game, right?

The House Built by Fear

Imagine living in constant fear. Feeling as if spirits were following and threatening you. There's a feeling you must spend immense amounts of time and money just to appease them. This is how Sarah Winchester lived for 38 years until she passed away in 1922.

Consultation After Tragedy

In 1862, Sarah married William Winchester of the Winchester Repeating Arms company. They had one child who sadly passed away in 1866 at only 6 months old. A few short years later William also passed away from tuberculosis.

Sarah was very distraught and decided to see a psychic in Boston. The psychic told Sarah vengeful spirits of her family members deaths were brought on by of those killed by the rifle bearing her husband's name. She advised Sarah to move out West and begin building a home to protect herself from the ghosts.

Construction Begins

Sarah moved to San Jose California in 1884. She had a 20-million-dollar inheritance and a thousand dollar a day income. She bought an eight-room farmhouse and began building. There was no plan or blueprint. Workers built 24 hours a day and 7 days a week. Sarah wanted to make sure to confuse any "bad" spirits that may have followed her. Every night Mrs. Winchester would travel to her séance room to communicate with the spirits and decide upon new additions of the home. Traveling to the séance room alone was meant to be discouraging to any malicious spirits. She would push a button that would cause a panel to swing open, revealing another room, she would then climb out of a window that led to the top of a staircase, she would go down the steps and then up another staircase that led back to the floor she was originally on.

This was not the only trick to confuse evil spirits. Some columns in the home were built upside down. Rooms were remodeled often and torn down week after week. Stairs would lead to ceilings; doors would open into walls, and the famous door to nowhere that leads outside to a large drop. The house was nearly 7 stories at one time, but the San Francisco earthquake in 1906 caused great damage. Sarah was trapped in her bedroom for several hours. She felt the quake was a warning from the spirits that too much time and money was being spent on the front portion of the home. She boarded up 30 rooms as well as the front doors.

Number 13 and Frequent Spirits

Mrs. Winchester also had a bizarre obsession with the number 13. There are 13 gas jets in the ballroom chandelier, many windows have 13 panes, there are 13 bathrooms, there are 13 steps leading to the 13th bathroom and 13 wall panels prior to this bathroom. There are 13 hooks in the séance room and even her will was written in 13 parts and signed 13 times.

When Sarah passed away in her sleep in 1922 construction ended on the house. This once 8-room farmhouse now covered 6 acres, had 160 rooms, 6 kitchens, 13 bathrooms, 2,000 doors, 10,000 windows, 47 fireplaces, and 40 staircases. Found in her safe were locks of her husband and child's hair along with copies of their obituaries.

The house is currently open to the public as a museum. Ironically, it takes just as much around the clock effort to maintain. Some damage from the San Francisco quake has been left as pieces of history. Of course, ghost stories continue to hover throughout the home. Sarah herself is one of the most frequently sighted spirits as well as phantom workmen who seem to continue to come to build for Mrs. Winchester.

Guided tours will take you throughout the home and there has been a behind the scenes tour added since my last visit. I will have to make another trip to explore all I was unable to see before. This house must be seen to be believed.

The Stanley Hotel

Redrum, redrum! Horror movie fans will remember those words vividly from Stephen King's "The Shining", a story about a man who slowly loses his sanity as the caretaker of a large hotel named The Overlook. Did such a place really exist? A hotel filled with spirits and ghostly activity. King was partially inspired for the story while staying at the Stanley Hotel in Estes Park Colorado.

Once a Guest, Always a Guest

The Stanley Hotel was constructed after F.O Stanley was diagnosed with tuberculosis. His doctor advised him to take in the clean mountain air though he had a grim diagnosis of 6 months to live. F.O Stanley and his wife stayed in a friend's cabin in Estes Park and fell in love with the area. Soon his health even started to improve. The Stanley's built a home for themselves in the mountains and 3 years later bought the land upon which the Stanley Hotel sits. Construction was completed in 1909. Word traveled fast about this extravagant and isolated hotel and soon celebrities and even royalty were making reservations. The hotel holds 138 guest rooms.

Mr. Stanley passed away in 1940 and he is just one of the many spirits reported at the hotel. He has been seen in the lobby and billiard room, he has even been seen casually strolling through the bar area. There have been reports of the employees attempting to stop the apparition before he heads to the kitchen area but he simply disappears.

F. O's wife Flora is also seen. She often enjoyed playing the piano and guests report seeing the keys to her beloved piano moving with no one playing them. The faint sound of music can be heard at times with no apparent source. The couple can also be seen together, walking through the corridors or engaging in guest activities.

Room 418 seems to get the most reports of paranormal activity. Cleaning crews have reported strange noises coming from the room. There have been imprints seen on the bed as if someone is sitting though no one is there. The most frequent reports are of the sounds of children in the halls. Guests have reported hearing children laughing, running, playing and even rolling a ball all throughout the night. Once a couple checked out early and complained the children kept them awake all night. Upon inspection, the guests were assured that no children were staying on that floor at the time.

Lord Dunraven, who owned the property prior to the Stanley's purchase, is believed to haunt room 407. He has been seen standing in the corner and often turns the lights off and on. There have also been reports of him opening and closing the windows when he isn't busy peering through them when the room isn't occupied.

Inspiration Strikes

My favorite known ghost of this hotel is Elizabeth Wilson. She was a maid at the Stanley many years ago. In 1911, there was a power outage at the hotel due to a storm, so Elizabeth was going from room to room lighting the gas lamps. She was unaware of a gas leak on the second floor and when she arrived to light the lamp at room 217 there was a large explosion and the room was quickly engulfed in flames. The heat caused the floor to cave and she fell through. She survived and Mrs. Stanley did everything to make her comfortable after the incident. She gave the maid a promotion, a raise, and free rent at the Stanley. Elizabeth continued to do what she loved at the hotel, even after her death a few decades later. She will reportedly fold and put away guests clothing and if an unmarried couple is sharing a bed, she will try to stay between them to insure things stay proper.

In 1974 when Stephen King stayed at the hotel, it was the last day of the season, there were very few people in the huge hotel and it had a truly unsettling energy. That night he had a dream his young son was being chased down the hallways, screaming with a giant fire hose behind him. When he awoke, the inspiration for The Shining was born. By the way, Stephen King's room number was 217.

Tower of London

What ingredients do you need to make the perfect haunted location? How about a building that's over 900 years old, that was used as a prison, torture chamber, and where public executions were held. This gives us the Tower of London.

History in the Walls

Built by William the Conqueror in 1078, the Tower of London's main function was to be a palace. Several expansions were built in the 12th and 13th century. There are now 20 towers and different buildings from different periods in history. Many held prison cells. The White Tower held torture chambers, Tower Green held Royal executions, and Tower Hill held public executions, just to name a few. Therefore, it was inevitable that a place like this would conjure up some spirits.

Queen Ann

One of the most famous ghosts is that of Queen Ann Boleyn. She was married to King Henry the VIII. On May 19th, 1536, Ann was arrested for high treason and sent to Tower Green where she was beheaded. There are reports of her headless body roaming the grounds, carrying her head under her arm; she has also been seen in the chapel, leading a procession of people in ancient dress.

Two Princes

There is also the tragic story of the "two princes'". Edward the V was 12 years old and his brother Richard Duke of York was only 10 when they were sent to the Bloody Tower after being declared illegitimate by

Parliament. The children soon vanished and it was assumed they were murdered by the command of their uncle the Duke of Gloucester in 1483. Later in the early 15th century, the apparitions of 2 children were seen frequently gliding down the stairs holding hands or holding onto each other in terror. In 1674, workman found a chest that contained 2 small skeletons. They were believed to be the 2 princes and were given a royal burial.

The Countess

The execution of Margaret Pole, Countess of Salisbury, has been seen replaying itself repeatedly. She refused to place her head on the chopping block like a "commoner" and ran. She was chased by the executioner with his axe and eventually met her demise after several blows from behind.

King Henry's Armor

The room where King Henry the VIII's suit of armor is exhibited is said to contain a "crushing" feeling. A guard reported feeling a cloak thrown over him and when he attempted to free himself, the cloth was pulled tightly by an invisible attacker.

White Lady

The White tower is one of the oldest parts of the building and is believed to contain the ghost of the White Lady. She has been seen waving to people at the building on the opposite side and her perfume hangs heavy in the air at the entrance to the chapel.

Guy Fawkes and the Grey Lady

The screams of Guy Fawkes can be heard echoing throughout the tower just as real as they were when he was tortured before being hung, drawn and quartered. There is also the Grey Lady who is seen roaming the grounds, wearing mourning attire and only a black void where her face should be.

Animal Spirit

Animals have also been seen in the Tower. In January of 1815 at midnight a sentry witnessed a large bear emerge from a doorway. He lunged at it with his bayonet but it went right through the apparition. The sentry died a few months later reportedly from shock.

Waverly Hills

A haunting is often brought on by trauma. What place sees more trauma than a hospital? During the early 1900s there was an outbreak of the very contagious tuberculosis, also known as "white death". With no cure available at the time, the disease would claim entire families. One of the highest death rates was in Louisville Kentucky. In 1910, a hospital was built on a hill in Jefferson County with hopes of combating the disease. The hospital quickly became overcrowded, and in 1924, a new structure was started. Two years later, in 1926, Waverly Hills Sanatorium was opened.

Those That Could Not Be Cured

Though considered very advanced for its time, the hospital still saw many succumb to the disease. While searching for a cure, patients experienced "treatments" that were at times worse than the sickness itself. It was believed at the time that rest and fresh air were the best cures. Patients would be placed outside regardless of the weather. They even tried exposing a patient's lungs to ultraviolet light to try to stop bacteria from growing.

The many patients that did not survive would be sent down the "body chute", this tunnel for the dead bodies led from the hospital to the railroad tracks at the bottom of the hill. Using a motorized cable and rail system the bodies were lowered in secret to awaiting trains. The hospital staff knew it would be too traumatic for the surviving patients to see just how many were dying from this disease.

Poor Intentions and Permanent Residents

Tuberculosis began to decline by the late 1930s and by 1946 new medications began to get the disease under control. Waverly Hills was closed in 1961 but was reopened as Woodhaven Geriatrics Sanatorium. However, the patients in the old age home were mistreated and many ailments were treated with electroshock therapy. Budget cuts led to horrible conditions, this combined with patient mistreatment led to the facility closing for good in 1982.

Considering the rich history, illness, trauma, and death, it really is understandable why Waverly Hills is believed to be one of the most haunted locations in the U.S. While the patients and staff are physically long gone, many spirits seem to have remained. A man in a white coat can be seen on occasion as he walks to the kitchen and the smell of fresh baked bread is apparent, although anyone looking at the kitchen can easily see a forgotten dilapidated, room where no one has cooked anything for decades.

Room 502 is one of the most infamous. In 1928, the head nurse of the room was found dead. She had hung herself from a light fixture. There was a theory that she was pregnant out of wedlock and couldn't handle her depression. A few years later, in 1932, another nurse for the same room fell to her death from the roof patio. There has been speculation that an unseen force pushed her. Paranormal investigators who have visited this room have encountered shadows, and a voice that warns entrants to 'get out'.

On the third floor, there is the spirit of a little girl named Mary. She is believed to enjoy playing with a ball that will roll across the floor or down the stairs. She is reported to appear and continually repeats that she has no eyes. Mary is just one of the many full-bodied apparitions to be seen. Doctors, nurses, and patients can still be seen, voices and strange noises can be heard down the "body chute". There is also a distraught spirit, believed to be a former patient that can be seen running and screaming for help, her wrists bleeding. Perhaps one of the most disturbing stories is that of the "Creeper", a spirit that crawls from room to room, sometimes along the walls or ceilings. This particular spirit is said to feel very dark and non-human.

Waverly Hills is currently open for tours and is in the process of being restored. Some feel this may add to the paranormal activity. Spirits seem to be stirred whenever construction is taking place. Tour info and the restoration process can be viewed on the website http://www.therealwaverlyhills.com

Zozo

You know how it is, you're scanning the web looking for the latest in scary or bizarre happenings, and then something catches your interest and the next thing you know you find yourself in a spiral of stories and theories. However, there comes the rare occasion when several stories match exactly or are eerily similar. This is a rare occurrence in the paranormal community so when it does happen you can sense the universal excitement in the air.

Who Is This?

I came across this the other night. I can't even remember how I got there but soon I was reading story upon story of an entity that refers to itself as "Zozo" and usually presents itself during Ouija board sessions. The fascinating thing with these stories are the similarities; people of different ages, from different parts of the country and even from other parts of the world have had experiences with this entity and the entities associated with him/her. Most research points to contact with this entity being reported through Ouija board sessions for at least 30 years. The theories of who Zozo is go back much further, to the early 1800s.

Usually the reports start out the same, a few friends, having a good time, "playing" with the board just to see what, if anything will happen. If Zozo isn't the first to come through an entity called Lilly will start communication. Lilly is reported as being nice and sometimes even warning the participant about Zozo. She has said Zozo is her evil sister. There are theories that Zozo and Lilly are the same entity and this is just a game it likes to play. When Zozo does come forth, there are some differences in how the session will go. Some say it will humor the participant by answering questions but this soon gets frightening when it reveals very personal information no one else should know. Another common report is the entity will come through as very angry, threatening and violent, often manipulating the board or the planchette by making it hot to the touch or launching it away from the participants. This seems to happen most often if the person comes through as a skeptic or is being purposefully disrespectful. Zozo is known to control the board, often saying frightening things like promises of death. Another common report is of an entity called Mama, again, there are theories this is all the same entity. Mama will appear usually during a session, the planchette will just move to M A M A over and over again. This is believed to be a tactic used by Zozo to confuse and weaken the mental defenses to move on to even more intentions that are sinister. A popular theory is no matter whom the board says you're talking to, a common giveaway that you're talking to this entity is the movement of the planchette in a figure eight motion.

The creepy thing, in addition to the fact that so many people have contacted the same entity, is that the contact, once initiated, doesn't stop at the board. People who have talked with Zozo have reported very terrifying occurrences days, even weeks later. Vivid dreams, catatonic states, accidents, even deaths have been reported, and not just affecting the person who used the board but their families as well. This phenomenon has caught the attention of many people in the paranormal community including demonologists.

Demon or Publicity Stunt?

Is this a demon? Many have called it such, however, usually a demon will not give its name so readily, though there have been theories that Zozo is not really a single name but a name for the group of entities that accompany what seems to be the leader. Some have called Zozo more of an ancient Deity instead. Many have tried to find the source of the name, saying it is another name for the demon Pazuzu, that it is a rough translation from the ancient Basque language meaning crow or blackbird. Some suggest this is the 3-headed dog that guards the gates of Hell. A movie has been made about the encounters and there have been accusations that this is all just a wild publicity stunt to gain popularity for the project.

Depending upon the part of the world or religion involved, the theories of the identity of Zozo are seemingly endless. Yet each day more and more stories are told of encounters and experiences with this entity and they are all similar in one way or another. I have never been a fan of the Ouija board for this reason. You never know what kind of door you're going to open or who or what is going to come through. I know there are rules to follow or Ouija etiquette if you will, but in my opinion, it doesn't matter if you opened and closed the session properly. When something is strong enough to come in, the greater the possibility it won't want to leave and the greater amount of danger you and your loved ones could be in for a long while.

On a personal note, I've revised this article, on both my desktop and my laptop, and each device has frozen at least twice on this article alone.

Resources

History of Halloween
Ghosts, Demons and Spirits in Japanese Lore
10 Odd Ways People Protected Themselves From
Witchcraft
Séance
A Magician Among the Spirits: The Improbable Friendship
of Harry Houdini & Sir Arthur Conan Doyle
Why the Devils Hour is so Terrifying
Victorian Mourning Etiquette
Victorian Monsters
Witchipedia
Mirror Mirror on the Wall: The Art and History of Scrying
Dream Magick
Necromancy: The Dark History of Raising the Dead
All About Poppets (Voodoo dolls)
Candle Magic
The Magic of Animals
Bloody Mary (folklore)
Bloody Mary Legend
Scary For Kids
Repleh Snatas Walkthrough!
5 Supposedly CURSED YouTube Videos!
Creepypasta Funnymouth
Annabelle the Demonic Doll: The True Story Behind the
Hollywood Legend
Clinton Road: A Dark Ride
The Strange and Mysterious History of the Ouija Board
Double Vision: The Strange Case of Emilie Sagee
Bad Omen #1: Lincoln's Doppelganger
A Ghostly Warning that Could Have Saved Sharon Tate
Sign of the Times... Tragic Suicide Off the H: 1932
The Hollywood Roosevelt Hotel – HauntedHouses.com

Author's Bio

Winter Balefire is an Author, Poet, Paranormal Researcher, and Occultist from Los Angeles, CA. Her articles on the paranormal, magic, lore, and urban legends have been continuously published since 2009 and she has been the subject of interviews in these areas. Winter loves to explore the dark and macabre. She has a passion for focusing on the topics that are considered taboo in hopes of educating the public on what is commonly misunderstood about the Occult. In December 2016, Winter's other passion, poetry, was brought to the world in her book *Love Letters Destroyed*. Her poetry was previously published in the Lovecraft themed, *Asylum Of the Ancient Ones,* and in mid-2017 was featured in an anthology called, *California's Best Emerging Poets*. Upon the release of her second book, *On A Ghostly Winter's Night*, Winter is continuing to research and write about the paranormal and Occult in hopes of shedding new light, decreasing fear and increasing understanding.

Winter's Social Links:
Winter Balefire's Webpage
Winter Balefire at Pseudosynth Press Publishing
Winter Balefire on Facebook
Winter Balefire on Instagram
Winter Balefire on LinkedIn
Winter Balefire at AllAuthor

Mr. Crowley

"Mr. Crowley"

[Daisley - Osbourne - Rhoads]

Mr. Crowley, what went on in your head?
Oh, Mr. Crowley, did you talk to the dead?
Your life style to me seemed so tragic
With the thrill of it all
You fooled all the people with magic
Yeah, you waited on Satan's call

Mr. Charming, did you think you were pure?
Mr. Alarming, in nocturnal rapport
Uncovering things that were sacred
Manifest on this Earth
Conceived in the eye of a secret
And they scattered the afterbirth

Mr. Crowley, won't you ride my white horse?
Mr. Crowley, it's symbolic, of course
Approaching a time that is classic
I hear that maidens call
Approaching a time that is drastic
Standing with their backs to the wall

Was it polemically sent
I want to know what you meant
I want to know, I want to know what you meant, yeah

Writer(s): Randy Rhoads, Robert John Daisley, John Osbourne